LIFE THAT NEVER ENDS

Petra ~ Christabel ~ Myself

This book is dedicated to my beautiful wife Petra and daughter Christabel, without their endless love and continual support I probably would not be here.
My love and deep appreciation also extends out to Grahame Bennett, Terry Linden-Fermor, and Peter Kong, as without their dedication this book could not be brought into existence

Dedication

This book is dedicated to my beautiful wife Petra and daughter Christabel, without their endless love and continual support I probably would not be here. My love and deep appreciation also extends out to Grahame Bennett, Terry Linden-Fermor, and Peter Kong, as without their dedication this book could not be brought into existence.

This Book is dedicated to my **Heavenly True Parents** who exist on earth and in the spirit world, resonating simultaneously together as one. Without them appearing on earth, none of this precious spiritual knowledge and understanding would have been revealed in such a clear and substantial way to many in this special historical time we all live in.

My humble desire in producing this book is to help others become aware of how the physical world and spirit world resonate and function in harmony together with the hope of helping others gain a clearer understanding of how the **Divine Principles** can work in their lives.

Share What I have learned over the years

The purpose of this book is to convey what I have learnt over many years of entering a person's spirit realm, and discovering and helping them solve different spiritual problems through giving them my spiritual readings.

All of these spiritual readings are from real-life requests that I have performed over many years with individuals and families. The readings have been converted into testimonies with the names, times and places erased or changed to ensure confidentiality and privacy of the parties involved.

As the reader, I would focus only on the request given me with descriptions of the problem and the influence it was having on the individual or family. Descriptions of why it was happening to them were given along with suggested ways to help them solve the problem.

Articles in **Part 1** of the book describe different realms in the spirit world which can act as references in understanding the collection of Testimonies in **Part 2** of the book. The collection of testimonies describe how ancestors and spirits are able to enter and occupy a person's spirit, whereupon they can then resonate and take root in the mind, body and spirit of the person and cause a positive or negative influence.

Through reading this book you may discover that problems or concerns you or others are experiencing might resonate with a particular reading; if this is the case, the suggested ways to help reduce or solve the problem at the end of each reading may be helpful.

The book gives clear descriptions of how the spirit world functions, allowing the reader to gain peace-of-mind knowing that their loved ones are waiting to receive them upon entering the spirit world when they are called to go.

Contents

Part One

Part Two

Philip Hill

Article 1

Introduction

The first part of this book will be a number of articles describing my experiences over several years showing the reality of the spirit world.

Spirit world has always been a reality for me from a very early age. But, my experiences of the spirit world were more of a burden and curse for me as I did not understand what I was experiencing.

I was (and continue to be) able to see spirits and communicate with them, and also to see the different areas that people go to and live in the spirit world. I unknowingly entered and observed how the spirit world was governed by absolute spiritual laws.

As I continued to observe, I realized that there is a system in the spirit world that determines how spirits continue to live and develop, and how they communicate with each other and with those closest to them on earth. This all seemed, on the one hand, quite natural but on the other hand felt very strange to me as I didn't have much life experience at that time.

Over the years I realized, through my experiences of observing these governing laws in action, that I could come to understand the connection and resonance between the physical body and the spirit body, and also the overlap of this physical world into the world of spirit where everyone eventually will end up.

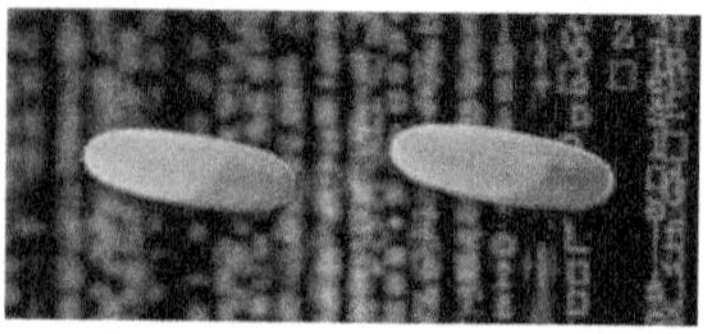

There is a metaphor being used in this modern time to describe the chaotic and sometimes confusing reality we are living in. In this modern, technological computer age more people than ever before, from all backgrounds and ages, are beginning to question and search for why they exist and what the purpose is for their existence. Many are now beginning to realize that there is more to what we see all around us; things that influence all of us in our daily lives.

There are different ways of describing what is going on in today's society, but the one I prefer to choose is one from the movie trilogy The Matrix, which in the first film focuses on a choice for the lead character between a blue pill and a red pill. The blue pill existence allows you to live your life as it always has been for many years, allowing you to go about your daily life in a very simplistic way. The red pill allows you to see behind the workings of general life and see how man is being manipulated in different ways to conform to the structure of a created society.

You are made aware of the reality behind what the population generally understands. This, in itself, becomes an awakening to the individual's true reality of how the manipulation of outside sources is completely out of their control. They realize that they are not even aware of how it is running the society and their individuals lives.

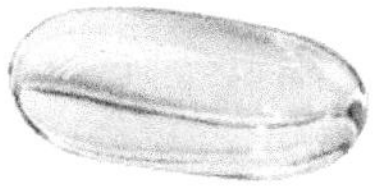

What the majority of the general public doesn't understand is that there is a third reality hidden beneath the 'red pill concept' which I would like to call the white or translucent pill. When this pill is taken, it opens your eyes not just to the way society is being dominated or influenced but also reveals to you the reality of the unseen world of spirit that ultimately influences our individual actions and decisions in our physical society.

This is the world I will be describing through my experiences; how each person is continually being influenced by their ancestors, those people that came before them, plus different spirits that have good or bad intentions. These all take a role in shaping how people see their surroundings and their place in this physical reality.

I had (metaphorically) taken the white pill at an early age, which opened my eyes to the reality of the spirit world. I entered into this invisible world and observed ancestors and different spirits, each with their own history. Many of these spirits that I observed were positive while others held resentments toward people on earth for the bad actions of their own ancestors.

I will be describing where ancestors dwell, and how we are influenced throughout our daily lives by them. I will also describe how negative spirits play a large part in causing frustration by blocking any progress being made by the individual.

There is a constant battle between the good ancestors we all have and negative or resentful spirits. Our good ancestors are always trying to protect their descendants from those negative influences. The following articles will go into detail about ancestors in general, what determines where they end up in the spirit world after leaving this earth, plus how spirits become negative or resentful and why they want to cause chaos for many living in the physical world.

What I have also become aware of through these many years as I entered into the spirit world each time is that there are absolute laws that determine how the spirit world works. There is nothing abstract about the spirit world, just as in the physical world nothing is abstract. Everything there is governed by natural law and order that allows the created world to continue to exist.

I will, over this series of articles, describe how these two worlds blend and work together to form a positive meaning of existence. I have observed that how people live their lives determines where they go in the spirit world. I will go into this reality in more detail since *knowing this will give each individual person a choice as to the way they live their lives in order to secure themselves the preferred area of the spirit world they will want to eventually live in after their physical body passes away.*

What many people don't realize is that we are living half in the spirit world already. Your physical body has a spirit body and these two resonate in harmony with each other. The spirit body allows ancestors and spirits to enter and occupy your spirit. And, as it resonates in harmony with your physical body, those ancestors and spirits are able to be absorbed directly into your physical body. Spiritual laws determine how people are influenced by ancestors and spirits, plus the atmospheres formed by positive or negative spiritual energy that people experience.

The universal intelligence and creative energy that caused existence to happen in the first place has many names. But, the most important observation I have seen is that no matter what name you put to the reality of this physical world and spirit world, the laws are the same and cannot be manipulated. It is outside of man's control and ability to change the way the natural physical and spiritual laws work.

I have observed different areas in the spirit world. Each of these could be called 'realms' or separate places where different groups of people with similar attitudes and outlooks on life dwell together. Each realm has large groups of people who have the same mindset and outlook on life as they had when they lived on earth.

One of the differences between the physical world and the spirit world is that in the physical world many different kinds of people all dwell together; different cultures, different religious backgrounds, different mindsets, all dwelling together here in one place on the earth.

Each person having different ideas and experiences they have gathered as they went through their life make a wealth of different experiences that can be shared. Being together here on this planet allows each individual to learn and develop the direction they want to go, often through the shared support and influence of others around them.

The input of others around us may suggest ways an individual can improve or be helped with different ideas or projects that could be shared together as a group. People around you can help shape the way you are able to develop and move forward in your life. Being able to share with people who have different ideas allows the individual to learn and grow and understand things they would

never understand without an outside alternative input.
At the end of one's life, you can either feel that it's been fruitful as your life developed from one understanding into possibly many that benefited you or, on the other hand, that it's been detrimental wherein the people you've taken advice and direction from may not have been so trustworthy and guided you in wrong directions which may have changed your life in seriously negative ways with a bad outcome.
So it is a 'double-edged sword' to live in this world surrounded by many who have different ideas and life experiences. It can become a lottery for us; being able to meet the right person or group of people that can help you in a positive direction, or the reverse which may shape your life in several unexpected and negative ways.
Through my observations I can see that the 'Creator' manifested this physical world in three dimensions; the same with the solar system and the entire universe also being three dimensional. Because of this, man's ability to live and create within this world is also influenced by three-dimensions. Life experiences are therefore limited as people can only produce experiences based on the laws of earthly time along with the knowledge that the body will die one day.
I observe that how people live here on earth and the experiences they gain are absorbed into their spirit body which then resonates

and accompanies each of them from birth till the end of their physical life. All those experiences accumulate and become absorbed into their spirit.

At the point where the body dies and passes away, your spirit which has accumulated all of your 'life experiences' along with your consciousness and self-awareness, naturally detaches itself from your physical body. Having served its purpose to gain experience's and to form your individual personality, your physical body then returns to the earth from which it came.

How you live and all the experiences you had throughout your life are retained within your spirit body and at this point, without your physical body, your spirit body naturally dwells completely in the spirit world. Your spirit body has always existed in the spirit world and resonated in harmony with your physical body, allowing it to absorb the experiences you had throughout your physical life.

The body's purpose is to form who you are through 'life experiences' in preparation for the next phase of your life which is to live consciously with all the awareness you had on the earth of who you are. But, once your life has transferred into the spirit world. the resonance of your physical body is severed.

This can be compared to the umbilical cord that connects the baby to the mother which, when the baby is born into the world, the umbilical cord is severed allowing the child to develop independently from the mother, but with all the attributes absorbed into the child from the mother.

You absorb all of 'who you are,' your physical life experiences and awareness, into the other half of yourself which is your spirit. You could say that your spirit is your 'second self' with all the awareness of how you lived on earth. This is the process of how the spirit detaches itself from the physical body and continues to live in the spirit world.

In my next article I will continue to share my observations of having watched many people's spirit disengage from their physical bodies and appear in the spirit world. I will describe the 'area' where you will first appear, what happens at that point and how it will be determined which area or 'realm' you are destined to go to.

Article 2

Following on from the previous article I will now share my observations of where a person's spirit body that has separated from its physical body appears, what procedures are used to enter into the spirit world and what determines the place or realm it will end up living in.

Using the metaphor of the white pill as discussed in the previous article, my spiritual senses have become open to the reality and activities in the spirit world and are able to observe what is happening behind the activities of the world we all live in.

In the picture above, a deceased person who has passed away lies in the casket in a church in front of relatives who knew him. The atmosphere is somber as there is a sense of loss of a loved one, which is quite natural and undcrstandable.

What the audience cannot see is that the spirit of the deceased stood behind the casket as can be seen in the picture. The spirit of the person looks to be wearing a white robe, but closer observation reveals that he is in fact generating intense white love energy which radiates out from within himself.

Being liberated from the physical body and all of its age complications allows the spirit to be free from many restrictions that would hold the spirit back. Each person has a root source of energy. This energy is your life element which originates from the "Creator," regardless of which name you may call it by. Each person is connected to this root source of vitality elements or life element.

Universal life elements enter through the center of your spirit just below the navel. Your spirit does not have a naval or any earthly organs but this is where it enters. From there the energy radiates out to the edges of your spirit body, making you appear extremely spiritually bright and giving the impression you wear a white robe. The body in the casket died from health complications around the age of 55, but the age of the spirit of that person standing behind the casket looks younger, around the age of 25. It is a well-known fact that people feel spiritually much younger than they actually are. When the body disengages from the spirit, your spirit expresses its optimal age.

Your body and spirit resonate together as you go through life growing, developing and experiencing things on a daily basis. As the body reaches the age of around 25, your spirit reaches its development potential but it continues to absorb life experiences. The spirit does not continue to age even though it continues to resonate with the physical body. Your physical body continues ageing past the age of 25 up until the time your body dies, which could be any age depending on your circumstances. The spirits of deceased people that I have observed all appear to look the age of around 25 years, more or less.

In the illustration, the spirits of the individuals you see standing on the steps behind the casket are relatives who expected his arrival and were ready to receive and guide the spirit of the deceased into the spirit world. The steps are symbolic. In the actual church, the casket is standing in front of a blank wall. The illustration shows the activities that are happening in the spirit world to receive the deceased and escort him into the spirit world.

The deceased spirit standing behind the casket looks out onto the audience. He is aware that they cannot see him. In his heart, of course, he feels sadness at leaving so many loved ones behind. But on the other hand, he feels completely free of the pain brought about through his aging.

At this stage he is also aware of how young and vibrant and full of life he now is. Being so full of vitality life elements, and having struggled for so many years with his physical health, it feels wonderful to have his zest back. He knows it will be a new beginning as he enters into the third phase of his life, living in the spirit world.

People have had dreams or visions that describe many different ways that a person enters the spirit world, such as steps or tunnels as shown above. Each of us are born twice; first when we are physically born and travel through the birth canal out into this physical world, and second when we travel through a tunnel or steps that naturally materialize at the end of our physical lives here on earth. Each process serves the same purpose as a way to enter the next life and world from the previous one.

If you have relatives who know you are coming, then the welcoming process to the spirit world can be different. The tunnel or spiritual birth canal depicted above is less personal with few preparations to receive you until you enter into the light that awaits you at the end of the tunnel.

The first picture shows that the deceased person's relatives were aware that the person was coming to the spirit world at that time and had two representatives waiting to welcome him. This is the difference between prepared and unprepared situations of spirits beginning their journey into the spirit world.

I have also observed spirits traveling through this spiritual tunnel or birth canal. Many other people who have had near-death experiences have described a dazzling bright light at the end of a tunnel. The person's spirit is drawn towards the light, either being transported or walking to the end of the tunnel. Having reached the end of the tunnel, the spirit then steps out into the bright light and immediately becomes enveloped in this intensely bright energy, the area he steps onto is a waiting area where a relative will meet the deceased to give comfort. Preparation will then begin as to which area the spirit will be guided too.

I will continue describing what I see happening from the first picture. As the earthly ceremony finishes in the church, the spirit of the deceased standing behind the casket is approached by the two representative relatives who passed into the spirit world a few years before him. They greet each other, offering kind and welcoming words to the deceased spirit. They all then turn and walk up the steps together and into an extremely bright area wherein the decision is made as to where that spirit will go and live; the same as in the second picture showing a tunnel.

Different experiential backgrounds, due to how they lived on earth, determine where each person's spirit will go. The waiting area, being extremely bright, is important as the purity of love residing in the atmosphere of the spirit world reveals the full history of your life experiences before your very eyes. Nothing is hidden as the memories of your earthly life come to the surface to be seen as clear as when each event happened.

This 'recollection process' is instantaneous, and with this memory awareness the correct place that is compatible with your own lifestyle and desires can be immediately found. There are countless areas or 'realms' all throughout the spirit world that can emulate your character and lifestyle. This being the case, it doesn't take long to find the appropriate match that you can easily fit into.

When you look out from earth into space, and if you can imagine seeing no planets or stars, then that is how vast the spirit world is. The spirit world is also multi-dimensional, which I will speak about in later articles.

From what I have been observing, the Creator who designed

existence has a parental heart wanting to give each person entering into this new exciting spirit world exactly what that person wants. It looks like the mind behind creation wants to make each person happy and comfortable by allowing him to live in an area or realm surrounded by people who had the same or similar outlooks and lifestyle.

The same process of entering into the spirit world happens to everyone. I have observed that entering the spirit world reveals there is a system and spiritual laws governing and directing the procedures. It also reveals that how you have lived your life and the lifestyle you chose determines where you end up in the spirit world, which is a serious realization.

The many areas or realms that are throughout the spirit world are all very different. For example, there are many different religious groups, each representing the earthly denominations. They are far apart and a 'no witnessing rule' keeps these congregations separated.

The physical world is made up of many different organizations, factories, office departments, dock yards, basically all that represents society as we know it. This is also represented in the spirit world in separated realms, which means anyone entering the spirit world would be guided to one of these areas that is most compatible to them.

Inside these realms there are complete towns and cities, both large and small. The layout of a town or city appears just as it does here on earth. I have often entered into different realms and observed similar social activities going on as here on earth, such as spirits of people going about their daily business, houses, shops and roads with street lamps; some days are sunny, some overcast or rainy, just as it happens here on earth. The difference being that in each of these spirit realms, the spirit of every one of the people living there is similar to all the others, whereas on the earth each person in any given area is totally individual and different. This is a serious distinction as it forms the framework for how a spirit can progress or remain stagnant.

I have explained that the individual lifestyle you lead determines what realm you end up in. For example, if your interest has been in living a Catholic lifestyle, then you will naturally be matched to one of the Catholic realms that suits your particular Catholic trend, as not all are the same. This also goes for those who conform to a protestant Christian lifestyle or any other religion, each having its different realm and different lifestyles that suits the individual. In fact, any lifestyle you can imagine has a realm that you can be matched to in order to accommodate your character. There you will be surrounded by similar like-minded spirits who on earth lived an almost identical lifestyle, which will make you feel comfortable in your surroundings.

The spirit world is eternal and so living in one of these spirit realms is a serious point to consider. Will a married couple end up living together in the same realm when they both eventually come to enter the spirit world?

Another important and serious point to consider is that you may end up being guided to a realm you don't want to be in, even though your lifestyle guided you to this realm. So, the question to be answered is, *"What choice do I have or what needs to happen to be able to change the realm I end up in?"*

These are the topics that I will cover in article 3.

Article 3

As stated in the previous article, if you are married, will you end up living as a couple in the same realm together when you both eventually come to enter the spirit world?

The other important point which can be quite serious is that you may end up being matched to a realm that you don't want to be in, even though your lifestyle and the way you've been living on earth guides you to it. So, the question to be answered is what choice do I have or what needs to happen to be able to change the realm I end up in?

To answer these important questions, I will describe my observations of the person's spirit standing behind the casket in the previous article. As you recall, he was met by two of his relatives on the steps, who at the end of the church ceremony guided him into the spirit world. These two topics covers a lot of content and will need to be extended over several articles.

I will use the relatives who guided the man into the spirit world as a third party to explain to him what is happening to him. All the following information you are about to read is a sample compilation of the spiritual experiences I am constantly observing. For the sake of clarity and not to cause any confusion, the body of the man behind the casket *has just recently* died and now his spirit body has entered the spirit world. Each person's spirit body in the spirit world appears solid, just like the physical body does on earth. Therefore, I will refer to a person's spirit body which appears in the spirit world as “him” or “her.” I wanted to clarify that as it makes the explanations much easier to convey.

Having determined, through the memories and lifestyle which the man lead throughout his life on earth, the realm he will end up living in, I then observed the recently-deceased spirit entering through a doorway into the same surroundings the person lived in when he was alive on the earth.

The picture below shows the reality of the realm in the spirit world he ended up in, which was the same place he lived in for much of his life. This demonstrates how real and solid the spirit world is.

I observed him looking around his home, the exact place where he lived before he passed away. All the objects in the room and decor he could totally relate to. He walked back to the front door from which he entered and opened it. He could see the streets and other houses exactly as they had been when he lived in on earth.

I observed many other spirits of people going about their daily business; some in cars and some waiting for a bus. Far off in the distance I observe a small town looking identical to one on earth. He walked over to the spirits of people at the bus stop and greeted them.

At this point he became aware that the people, including himself, were wearing normal daily clothes just like on the earth. Everything felt so solid to the touch. His awareness and understanding of the spirit world completely changed as everything looked completely physical and so familiar.

He greeted the people at the bus stop, who responded in a courteous way. He said, “I have just arrived in my home where I have been living for several years on earth.” “Yes,” they said, “We know.” He then continued, saying “The neighborhood looks exactly as I left it.” They responded by saying, “Yes, we know you just arrived.” They said they had been living here a long time and pointed to their homes along the street.

He was surprised because he had never seen any of these people living in his immediate vicinity back on earth, so he asked them who they were. Through their conversation he realized that the character and temperament of those people speaking to him corresponded to his own. They all responded in a manner that was the same as his; each having lived a similar lifestyle and having the same ambitions as himself. He also realized they were of all nationalities; from different countries all around the earthly world. He could see that everyone in this realm could easily relate to each other as they all had similar backgrounds and lifestyle. He was curious to know if anyone had seen any other realms in the spirit world. They said they had never seen anything outside of this realm.

He continued asking, "Have you ever travelled outside of this town to other cities?" "Yes," they said, "even to different countries. Every place we visited was identical to the ones seen on the earth; the same kind of weather, atmosphere, etc." They said the only difference each of them recognized was that each person they meet had the same outlook and lifestyle as themselves.

I observed him beginning to realize how vast the spirit world is. He thanked those people at the bus stop for sharing and informing him about their experiences and said he will probably see them around. He then turned and walked back to his house.

He walked through his home to the back door where on earth, at the back of his home, he could look out onto a large area of empty fields. He was curious to see if that was still possible. He was amazed as he looked out onto the horizon and could see the identical panorama that he had seen when on earth.

He made himself a cup of tea as everything was in the same place in his kitchen as it had been on earth. He knew where everything was. Everything was so real visually and to the touch. He realized it was not a dream and began to relax and wonder about his wife and children back in the physical reality.

He also wondered if, when the time would come for his wife to enter the spirit world, she would be coming to join him or not. At that instant he heard a knock on the front door. Upon opening it, he was greeted enthusiastically by one of the relatives he met on the steps at the funeral who had welcomed him and guided him into the spirit world.

I observed the relative being invited in, whereupon he was offered a drink and the two sat together. The conversation turned to his wife and children. He asked if the relative knew anything about whether his wife would be joining him as she was also getting older in age and would probably be passing away sometime in the near future.

The relative, who did not live in this same realm, answered him by saying "No. She will not be joining you here in this realm because the law was set up generations ago such that an agreement was signed by you at your marriage ceremony saying, at the point of death, you will separate and depart. This means that your wife will be guided to the realm that would suit her character and lifestyle. *'Till death us do part.'*"

I observed him becoming quite overwhelmed with sadness at this answer. He went on to ask, "Will I ever see her again, then?" The answer was "No." Things went very quiet. Pulling himself together he said, "Can I ask you some questions?" "Of course," was the answer. "Then can you tell me all that you know about what happened to me and what the future looks like for me?"

The relative said, "I will try my best to explain what I understand about this incredible place of the spirit world we are in. Please feel free to interrupted me to ask questions as it may make my job of explaining much easier."

He asked the relative what realm he was from and could he come and visit him in his realm. The relative said, "At this time you are not able too, but it is possible. I will need to explain a lot more to you so you can understand your reality at this point in time. Later, I will explain the process you would need to go through to become free of the restriction that ties you to this realm. So, please have patience."

"The process is available on earth, had you understood and lived accordingly, by which you could have already been freed from the ties of any of the spirit realms here. But, because that never happened, I will need to give you some general background. Then you will be able to make a choice whether or not to continue living in this realm or to take the opportunity to become free from the ties and spiritual restrictions you are now under. So, after I have finished explaining to the best of my ability, you can choose."

I observed the relative start explaining. He began by saying, "I can only explain what I myself understand, as it is not easy to fully understand everything. But, I will try." He began by saying, "Even though you were married, you separated at the point of death. Your wife will go through the same process on entering the spirit world that you did, and you will be there to meet her just as I met you. But, you won't be able to stay with her until you make the choice to become free as I explained before."

He continued: "Through her memories and lifestyle she will

likewise be matched to the realm that best suits her; where the people all have similar characteristics and outlooks so she can easily fit into the society there."

"I have a question," he said. "Before you begin, could my wife also be set free through what you are going to explain, or is that not possible?" The relative answered enthusiastically, "Yes, of course!" "Would this mean then that we could be together?" "Absolutely," answered the relative. He went on to say "It's also good that she is not coming here now, which gives you plenty of time to understand what living here is all about and how to take control of your own spiritual life."

He interrupted once more by asking, "How long will you be here with me and what if you wanted to stay here?" The relative answered: "This is where you will spend the rest of your existence. Each realm is completely different. But within each realm there is an eternal dimension which means, for example, that you can travel the world within each realm. This is how vast the spirit world is."

I observed the relative continuing to explain, "There are as many spirit realms as there are people on the earth, with each having their different characteristics which are compatible with the individual tastes and lifestyle of each person living on the earth."

He went on to say that the reason why there are so many people living in any particular realm is because all the people that went before us, throughout human history, eventually passed into the spirit world and ended up in their appropriate realm.

He continued to explain that the spirit world is multi-dimensional and the physical world has only three dimensions. He went on to say, "To understand why there is a difference, I will need to explain why you were born on earth first instead of coming directly to the spirit world." I observed the relative beginning to explain it in a simple way in order for him to make sense of what was happening to him.

He began by saying, "The Creator, however you want to call *'it'*, manifests law and order; physical laws and spiritual laws that work in the same way. But, physical reality has a different purpose than spiritual reality while the laws are the still the same."

He continued saying, "The process that brings a person into the physical world begins by being born through the mother's birth canal as you know, and out into the physical world. Each person enters the world generally this way; conceived by your parents. This is then *the first* birth process. This can happen in many different ways, but the egg and sperm originate from within two people, a man and a woman, ideally being the parents who are the root of the child's life. They contribute the source energy plus the inherited blueprint containing all characteristics of each parent. This allows the child to grow and flourish through the love of the parents or guardians."

I will continue this large topic in Article 4.

Article 4

Continuing on from article 3 and to keep you up-to-date...

I have symbolically taken the *white or translucent pill and* my senses have been opened so I can see clearly into the spirit world. I am continuing to observe spiritually a conversation between a man's relative who has been living in the spirit world for several years and his newly deceased family member. The relative is sharing and passing on his experiences to the man who has just died and is attempting to educate him about the reason people are born on earth first instead of being born directly into the spirit world.

Helping the *newly deceased* to understand what has happened to him, his relative sets out to explain what life is all about to the best of his ability and understanding, having lived in the spirit world himself for several years.

At this point in the conversation he continues by saying: "There are two stages each person will go through before the end of his or her life on earth and before entering and living in the spirit world. The first stage the baby develops in is within the mother; the realm of *water*. The baby inherits from the parents all the information that it will need to recognize and relate to the earthly world and be able to physically grow and develop through the nurturing of its parents.

The second stage of our physical life is the world of *air,* thereafter followed by the third and final stage, the world of *spirit.* The Creator manifested mankind in his image. The birth process, and the physical world with its three-dimensional laws allows you to experience earthly life and at the end of your life end up in the spirit world".

"This is a natural three stage process. The Creator created these three processes so that people can relate and experience life on the earth and, with those experiences, they can enter into and be able to relate to the spirit world."

He went on to explain that many people believe the spirit world to be completely abstract and unfathomable but this is not the case as the transition process from the physical world into

the spirit world, where every single person ends up, is a natural consequence and our final resting place.

"The Creator would never make a spirit world that is so abstract that people entering it would never understand it. It seems from my experience living here that the Creator wants to make his 'creation' happy by allowing people to take with them into the spirit world all their personal experiences so they can continue living the lifestyle they choose, or have a chance to change and develop a better life for themselves."

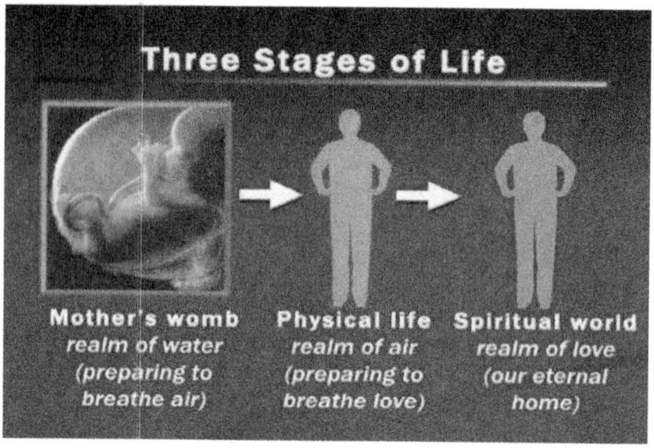

"Each of the three stages is a world all its own. The womb becomes your first existence. Being born and living in the physical world becomes your second existence. And, through gaining experiences of life, you take those memories and experiences with you into the third phase of your existence, that being the spirit world."

Your purpose living on the earth was not meant to last eternally. Your only purpose on earth was to gain experiences and become aware of who you are. As you gain those experiences, you discover your own limitations and successes, which allows you to become a unique individual with a personality.

The other purpose for living on earth is to marry and produce children who can continue in that world acting as a replacement for you, in order to carry on the lineage. I will talk about this from a spiritual point of view in future articles.

At the first breath a child takes, his spirit is formed. The body of the baby lives in the physical world while its spirit, which resonates in harmony with the body of the baby, at
the same time dwells in the spirit world. As the baby grows and experiences life, those experiences are absorbed directly into its spirit."

The relative goes on to say that each of us, male and female, have a spirit that resonates in harmony with our bodies. The purpose of the spirit is to absorb all the experiences you have through your life and also to guide you to become individually aware of who you are so the physical body can be allowed to die naturally. At that stage, the spirit disconnects from the physical body with no feeling of separation. Everything you were, before in your physical body, you remain now in your spirit body. Many people have been able to observe their own physical body just as the final physical life element finishes and watch from their spirit body as their spirit detaches itself.

This natural process allows you as an individual to continue living in the third phase of your life within the spirit world, with all the experiences you had and with full awareness of yourself. You then continue living your life. Developing your individuality is the purpose of the physical body. It does not need to live any longer than 100 years or so.

The body's only purpose is to allow you to become aware of yourself and form your personality with a variety of experiences so that you can live for eternity in the spirit world. So, it is like a chrysalis although it has a short lifespan. It is necessary for the development of the butterfly that time to form itself within is allowed before it breaks out and is set free into this physical world, but in man's case the spirit world.

The relative then went on to say that from what he understands, "The human race was originally meant to resonate with the Creator spiritually as we all come from the energy of the Creator. But, we became separated from the beginning of our existence, making individuals unaware of the reality of the spirit world and of their own personal spirit."

"Because of this people became directionless, not knowing the reason why they existed. Each person would have originally been informed of their purpose of existence by the Creator through the resonance we would have had with him/it if we had not become disconnected." Even today, people don't know why they exist or where they will end up after their physical life ends. The Creator's desire is to resonate once again within each of us as human beings."

"As you look back in history, attempts to inspire and guide the general public were made by different historical figures and people with vision. Many of them received spiritual insights into the purpose of life and went on to form various religious groups and organizations. They created laws and traditions that allowed people to find a common purpose and direction in their lives. The problem is that many of their teachings were somewhat extreme and prevented people from working together with other groups. This became a big problem over the many generations. However, without them there would have been no basic law and order in modern society today."

The relative continues, "This time in the 21st century, humanity is reaching a crossroads or pinnacle where people are themselves becoming aware of the presence of an invisible world. Even some scientists are aware of law and order in nature which is not coincidental."

"They know there is intelligence behind nature that is governing our existence here in the physical world. They also know that whatever intelligence *is* guiding and forming this physical world, it must be from a world that cannot be seen directly but is able to be recognized and recorded on different scientific instruments."

Many people have had near-death experiences wherein their body almost died as they witnessed their spirit separating from their body and they were able to see into the spirit world. With many people having the experience of seeing a bright light at the end of a tunnel and even traveling to and stepping out into that light, as I have described in a previous article.

"The time we are now living in is a crossroads; a pinnacle of learning and experience where people are more-than-ever able to directly connect with and resonate in harmony with different experiences of the spirit world. Because of this special time, it's important to be able to free oneself from the old theological traditions and shackles that trap people in narrow-minded thinking. All the experiences you gain on earth are based on countless inherited traditions and lifestyles which each person has also become trapped in. Your narrow-minded thinking prevents you from being able to harmonize with others who are also trapped in their narrow-minded views and lifestyle."

"Each person entering the spirit world brings with them their narrow-minded thoughts, ideas, experiences and individualism which is why there are so many different realms. People in general, on the earth, often cannot unite with each other because of these narrow-minded concepts which have no basis in reality. This was never the Creator's original plan for people."

The relative continues to explain "The Creators original idea was not to have any separate spirit realms, but for people to harmonize together as one big world family resonating with the physical and spiritual laws and creating harmony in yourself and with those around you." Because of people's growing awareness and awakening to the reality of a spirit world, it opens up a completely different understanding of why we are all here on earth and the direction we should go.

The physical world has three dimensions. Its sole purpose is to allow your physical body to experience life in an individual way and absorb those experiences into your spirit. For this to happen, three dimensions is enough. It becomes like your personal chrysalis that keeps you restricted to 3 dimensions.

At the time of spiritually disengaging from your physical body and from this earthly life, you become set free into the spirit world. You are ready to enter into a much higher dimension, a multidimensional spirit realm, which allows you infinite choices and experiences which are completely different from the restricted life experience you had on earth.

The relative continues to explain, "Each person is a unique being; the only one that ever existed. Also, you're eternal. So as you continue living your life in the spirit world and because of your ability to express in a unique way, the Creator gives you this multi-dimensional space to express your uniqueness. You have no restrictions in the spirit world. The problem, though, that most people have is that they are just not aware of this reality or that there is a *place* like that. They believe the spirit world is either heaven or hell, based on old theological traditions and narrow thinking. The parable of the 'blind leading the blind' can be used here," the relative continues speaking, with frustration.

He knows that if people could know and understand that the spirit world gives each person total freedom to express themselves, they would have a very different approach to how they live their lives here on earth. The person's lifestyle determines how limited they are or how free they are in the spirit world.

At this point the man asked his relative a question: "Is it even possible to explain this to people on the earth since they have such narrow-minded viewpoints which they probably inherited and since they are connected to so many narrow-minded organizations or groups? Is it still possible to help them see a new way? I ask because I never heard of or knew anything about what you are explaining to me before."

The relative answered saying, "It is possible. It's just a matter of education to explain the new spiritual understanding and principles discovered in this 21st century, making it one of the most exciting times to live in. People can be educated and given the chance to move out of the old history and burden they carry into a totally new understanding of their own reality."

The relative goes on to say that when people realize what their true purpose is on earth and where they are going physically and spiritually, they can consciously break out of their own narrow-minded thinking. People are quite creative in their own way and have the ability to change themselves if they have a good reason to do so.

I observe the relative explain: "This also applies here in the spirit world. The same process is used to allow you to free yourself from the narrow-minded ideas you brought with you into the spirit world, along with all the narrow-minded inherited ideas. All these narrow-minded, inherited ideas and concepts have caused so many historical problems for so many people on the earth and has kept them divided and unable to harmonize with one another, as explained before. It is possible to remove all those memories and narrow-minded, limited experience's here in the spirit world."

The relative goes on to say that he has done it himself. He went through the process and is, himself, now free to be able to travel anywhere in the spirit world. "I can visit any spirit realm and not be influenced or trapped by any of the realms characteristics. This is because I don't resonate with any of my old inherited concepts or traditions. This is the reason I could visit you here in this realm and not become trapped. Instead, I now harmonize and resonate only with the universal spiritual laws."

The universal laws that govern the physical world and spirit world originate from the Creator, however you wish to call *it*, whose energy and vitality elements continuously flow out from itself into everything that exists. The essence of this vitality element is love. When people are allowed to step outside of the narrow-minded theological history they each have, then they blend into the natural laws where they become an envelope of the Creator's vitality element of love.

The relative goes on to say, "This is how mankind should live. Each person has his own individuality and creativeness, but will also be able to resonate with the universal laws when living in the physical world. This in turn allows people to harmonize naturally with each other without conflict, continuing on into the spirit world in the same harmonious way."

"The original plan was to all resonate in an atmosphere of love. This was the idea that the Creator wanted to happen but it never did. All throughout history, constant effort has been made by the Creator to make this happen. Now is the time it can be accomplished."

The relative then followed, "You had another question such that if you ended up in a spirit realm you *didn't want* to be in, then what you could do to change your realm? I have explained that there is a method to becoming totally free of any connection or influence of any spirit realm; even this one."

"My hope," he said, "and desire, is to invite you to the place in the spirit world that I come from and become liberated from your old narrow-minded inherited history and traditions so that you don't need to remain in this realm. But before I do that, I will go on to describe the different atmospheres of positive and negative realms and explain the differences between them, plus the influences they have on the people who end up there."

Article 5

I will now go on to briefly describe the three different spirit realms I have visited and why they are so different. I will start by describing a positive realm, then middle realm, and finally lower realms.

There is another realm which is where restoration and liberation happens. In this realm it is possible to remove your old history, which will then allow you to leave your realm and be reunited with your wife or husband whom you were separated from at the time you passed into the spirit world.

This realm is spiritually unique and completely different in how it operates. I will describe my experiences of this realm in a testimony which follows.

A high (or positive) realm

The lifestyle lived on earth and the spiritual influences you inherited from your ancestors determine the actions you perform. If your ancestors lived a humble lifestyle and had a religious upbringing, you would inherit their good qualities of devotion or humility. These kind of ancestors are constantly seen around people on the earth. Many influential ancestors or spirits enter and occupy each person's own spirit to reinforce the ideas and actions of that person towards those around them. It is often said that a person looks and acts or thinks very similarly to their father or mother or grandfather or grandmother or some other relative.

Below is a picture of my wife. As she was talking, her parents appeared from the spirit world to support her vision and the way she expressed herself.

OCT 2001
Petra's grandmother and father visited to help inspire her while talking

The way you express yourself and the way you do things reveals the qualities of the ancestors that are with you. As you go through life gaining experiences with the support and guidance from your ancestors, your actions are absorbed into your spirit which then forms the foundation of who you are.

When your body passes away, you take into the spirit world all of those actions that become attracted to that particular spirit realm. If you live a humble, good life living for the sake of others and wanting to help within your family and community, then the realm you go to reflects those qualities, as with everyone in that realm.

When you live for others *unconditionally*, the Creator *resonates* with this. It's vitality elements of life energy, love, desire and purpose for creating life all were for people's enjoyment. Because of this when you, living on earth, want to live for others in your family and society, the Creator's love energy is attracted to your actions as you emulate the Creator himself.

The Creator's vitality element of love is extremely bright. As a person continues to go through life living unconditionally for others in many different ways, he accumulates memories of those actions and the bright spiritual vitality elements from the Creator. People having these kind of experiences can easily blend into the bright energy of love. The physical and spiritual laws of the universe emulate the Creator who created everything. Being able to blend into the bright energy of love within your spirit allows you to enter into the spirit

world through that channel of love. Even being old in age your spirit looks bright, making your whole physical appearance look much younger.

When people with those experiences enter the spirit world, they naturally become attracted to a bright spirit realm where the atmosphere of love is shared by all who dwell in that realm. Everything you see is bright and colorful. Each day feels like a summer day with a bright blue sky and a warm breeze.

All the houses in that realm have entrances without doors and large clear windows which allow the sun in and people to enter in easily and share things together. There is a lot of harmony and desire to help each other. There is no night; only warm sunny days accompanied by a wonderful peaceful atmosphere. This is a description of a spiritually high realm.

This is just one description of a large number of high spirit realms. They are all slightly different as each of us differs, having many different experiences. So, not all of the realms are the same.

The picture below also expresses this kind of spirit realm. Most good, kind-hearted people dwell in these realms which are classed as spiritually high-level realms.

Having lived a good life, mainly living for the sake of others in many different ways, you have attracted to you a high level of God's creative vitality elements that dwell in love.

God's love, being a creative energy, means for you that you can spiritually resonate in harmony with the root source of life and are able to create whatever you desire. God is a parent who wants to give his children everything. This is a wonderful thing because you can create your own environment to live in; one which you can enjoy the most.

Each person's environment can be as varied as his own creativity allows, which is why you see so many different interpretations or impressions of how the high spirit world looks. Each of those impressions are right, as everyone has a different mindset that pleases them. Thus, any number of different environments can be seen. No matter how abstract or normal looking they are, they are right for that individual person or couple.

Those couples who were married and lived together on the earth are not together in this realm immediately, as they were separated when they passed into the spirit world. One of the vows at a traditional wedding on earth was to live together "till death do you part." In the next testimony, article 6, I will describe the new realm that allows 'liberation' and the ability to leave your particular realm. This is where reunion of lost love ones can take place and as a couple you can then live together in your own desired area together.

Below is a picture of a wonderful and beautiful realm created by the individual living there.

Another picture below shows a fantasy world. This is also created by the individual or couple living there. Whatever and wherever you desired to live will manifest in that environment. Each individual in a couple has a strong bright spirit that radiates vitality elements. God can blend with that person's or couple's vitality elements. Using these vitality elements that resonate with God, our True Parent allows your environment and your desired possessions to manifest and be created just for you.

Even though you may not be immediately together with your love ones, there are other people who think the same way. So, you can still share your environment with others. It is difficult to advance your spiritual level since everyone is on a similar level with you. lived on the earth, this particular high realm is quite comfortable to live in.

But, because the level of love you took with you to the spirit world was a sacrificial love, expressed in many different ways when you Many people can feel energy from nature and often like to live in or near a forest, for example. In a natural way these people are attracted to *this* spirit realm. They feel most comfortable dwelling in an atmosphere of love. People who meditate or pray can easily harmonize within this realm.

The picture below expresses the heart of love from deep within the individual. This then becomes visible and creates the atmosphere and external environment that is comfortable for that person in this realm.

There is no "*time*" as we measure it on the earth, but only that

moment. You can develop and have experiences which are absorbed into your own spirit, but time doesn't pass the same as we understood it before. So, if you feel at peace in your heart, then that is how it will continue. Life without any form of torment is heaven for most people, which is why this realm is known as a spiritually high realm.

I will now give a brief description of having visited a middle spirit realm, and explain the different atmospheres it has and the type of people who dwell there.

There are *middle realms* that look very similar to the physical places you lived in on earth. One of these realms I described in a previous article wherein the man was guided into the spirit world by his relative and ended up in a *middle realm*. These have all the characteristics of your general neighborhood, city or town.

The atmosphere in these realms can change depending on how changeable you yourself are, as well as the others that dwell in this realm. If you feel happy, the atmosphere reflects your mood and becomes bright. If you feel, sad the atmosphere reflects that mood and becomes dull or gray, or it can even begin to rain!

If you were a changeable person who had mood swings when living on the earth, then this is reflected in the spirit realm you live in. The middle spirit realm is by far the largest realm. Most people on the earth who have lived a plain, regular lifestyle or can even be said to have lived a *neutral lifestyle* accumulated these kind of memories and experiences. They may have shallow mood swings that change the atmosphere around them mildly, but constantly. The way this works is that each individual person influences their own atmosphere and does not affect their neighbors'. This is similar to what happens on the earth, with each living their individual lives with their own individual ups-and-downs of emotion, separated by the homes they live in.

The picture below shows a typical row of houses in a middle spirit realm, with each resident living individually in each house surrounded by all the things they recognize when they lived on the earth. Each person having a different temperament or outlook on life creates the atmosphere surrounding that individual. This also explains why the spirit world is multi-dimensional as each person within that realm has their own individual realm they live in.

Each person on the earth lives in their own different world. One way to describe this is when you see a large crowd of people you see them all in the same place, but within each person they have a different mind and spirit. Because each of them has a spirit body they can each dwell in a different reality within themselves, but externally they all appear in the same place as you look at the crowd.

This is possible because the spirit world is multi-dimensional and able to incorporate every single person's different memories and characteristics. The physical body on earth has three dimensions which keep the mind and spirit contained. When the body passes away, the spirit becomes free and blends into the multi-dimensional spirit world which then increases in size creating a whole new environment and surrounding for yourself. This environment can be as vast in size as you want.

God, our True Parent, wants to make each individual person happy as we are all his children. This is why the spirit world is multi-dimensional and able to allow people their individual freedom to live the way they want to. Because several people may have the same lifestyle, they can possibly end up all living in the same realm. This is why there are so many people living together with the same lifestyle, as many people have the same outlook on life.

The middle realm is like an earthly realm. It's very similar, with the same kind of characteristics. The people living there also express similar characteristics as described above. The reason for the mood swings that effect your individual environment is because of the experiences you had on earth. By being supported by your ancestors, those who want to support you, they can be both helpful and/or also cause problems by limiting you.

Our ancestry goes back over thousands of generations. If your ancestors lived a meaningful life, being good and kindhearted folks, they would have developed a bright enough spiritual level to attract Gods pure vitality elements to them. Being sociable and enjoying the company of others, many would gather together in their homes or social clubs, pubs and so on. Many dedicated themselves and helped others, such as in the case of doctors, nurses or firemen, or they may have done police work, Red Cross, volunteer workers, etc., all willing to give their lives for others. Care workers also all fall into this category.

Different kinds of *selfless giving* can cause different degrees of mood and atmosphere, being neither positive nor negative but rather taking a middle, level-headed approach to life. This is why they end up in this middle realm which is the largest realm.

People who have a strong religious connection and have been devout church-goers don't necessarily have a connection to the higher spirit realms but tend to focus on the ideas and hopes that their particular church, organization or community offered them. They had *hope* as a family or community, but can be quite narrow-minded in their desire to expand their minds. Instead, these people believed unconditionally what they were told or read and strongly believed what their theology taught them in a blind way. This attitude they took with them into the spirit world. There they all gather together in their chosen spirit realm, devoted to their particular doctrines and unable to see outside of their own ideas or lifestyle.

These people are truly trapped in their spirit realm, unable to advance spiritually. This is so sad because the spirit world has no restrictions, leaving you free to be as creative as you like. But, having such a narrow mindset on earth, they prevent themselves from experiencing the wonders of this new world. The whole purpose of religions was to free mankind from the earthly dominance that material possessions can have on you and help give you a way of understanding that living unconditionally, in service to others, attracts to you Gods creative vitality elements of love. When you enter the spirit world all you bring with you is your spirit body and the vitality elements of love you gained from living for others, which emulates God.

Focusing on this aspect of your life brings true value, allowing you to connect with and blend into God's pure environment of love in the spirit world where all things become possible. God, our parent, is then able to give you what you desire as you blend into his creative vitality elements of love. Religions were meant to educate people, but often failed. People having free will often connect in a possessive way to their earthly belongings and ideas. This creates for them a spiritual block, trapping them and preventing them from living any kind of unconditional lifestyle towards others. This spiritual limitation they will then take with them to the spirit world. Even though people living here are limited, their profession or care-work did help them to develop a certain degree of selfless attitude. God can use these experiences to help give them a positive place to live in even though they won't have much control over obtaining what they truly desire.

Couples are not seen in this world. There are only individuals dwelling here.

I will now give a brief description of the lower level spirit realms I have visited, the atmosphere they have and what kind of people end up there. I will describe in greater detail more about negative and resentful spirits and how they manipulate people in further testimonies.

This realm is cold, dark and damp with a heavy overcast, depressive atmosphere where fear, suspicion and anxiety dwell.

This realm is a very dangerous realm for anyone who has not been liberated from their own burden of fallen history. The reason is that the atmosphere, being so bad and destructive, will stick to any negative experiences you carry subconsciously within you on earth. The negative atmosphere will stick to you and blend into your spirit, amplifying those bad experiences you carry and making them become overwhelming for you. You will then become lost and trapped in your negative experiences, not being able to find your way out. This can lead to nervous breakdowns, suicide, or extreme loss of hope and purpose to continue living on earth as you become overwhelmed with depression.

People on earth mostly experience this realm from being visited by negative or resentful spirits that are allowed to torment them because of the bad actions a few of that person's ancestors caused to others when they lived on earth. You being the descendent of those ancestors means that you have the *base* of their bad action inherited from them. I will describe this process and the influences they have in greater detail in further testimonies.

Ancestors and spirits in this realm are strictly segregated and suffering. The enjoyment of torture towards other ancestors and spirits creates an atmosphere of terror as different torture methods inflict 'pain' continually. Dungeons are a common sight, plus many more indescribable dark, cold places of suffering and torment that are unable to be entered. These all exist within this realm.

People that were killed become intensely resentful and search for the ancestor that killed or tortured them. They then get great pleasure from inflicting pain and torment on the perpetrator. Having no physical body, the *pain* is more in the mind of the ancestor or spirit being tortured. The spirit body cannot 'die' from being tortured or killed. The hell for them is that there is no escape from being tormented by the person he/she killed or tortured; this is the hell.

People on the earth that kill others or even themselves, such as suicide bombers, are in an even worst position as they enter the spirit world. They are guided to this low, dark realm and become surrounded by others like themselves. Here they continually blow themselves apart. The innocent victims are guided to different, better realms and are given the freedom to visit their killer if they so desire. This is because they may have developed intense resentment towards them so they want to go to them in order to also torment them. This becomes a double hell for the killer.

The reason for the segregation of this low realm of darkness into 'multiple different realms' is because there are so many different extreme cases there. Below are a few pictures of this reality to give you some impression of how it looks and would feel. Spirits in this realm own nothing and have no thought for anyone accept themselves. God's creative vitality elements of love do not exist or only to a very small degree, which is why they own nothing. God would like to give them everything but is unable to blend into their spirit as they have no usable vitality elements. Also, God cannot acknowledge anything evil and must leave them to look after themselves *or* until they can be released through the spirit body of someone attending a 'liberation program.' I will talk more about that later on.

In order for any progress to be made for ancestors in this realm, only an ancestor from the highest level spirit realm that has been 'liberated and Blessed' can visit this realm and offer the chance to that particular ancestor who has been requested to be found by one of their descendants now living on the earth. Anyone else visiting this dark realm would become trapped and unable to leave.

Below are two ancestors existing next to a particular building from a time when they lived on earth. They don't want to leave it, as it holds many memories. It may be from fear of spiritually moving on to another spiritual level. So, they can become trapped in this realm of existence where they may stay completely unaware of time passing, meaning they may have been there for centuries.

This person below is set to wander in the building she may have been murdered in. She may not even be aware that she has died as often the intense horror of the experience fixes your mind to block out all other reality. She believes she is still alive in the building she recognizes and has lived in on earth, which demonstrates how real and solid the spirit world is.

Below shows a ship graveyard where many sailors died but they will continue to occupy it. They don't want to move on spiritually and so remain together with their ship. This means they could be there eternally, as time doesn't pass like it does here on earth.

I will now conclude my descriptions of these different realms. As the testimonies progress, it is important to have a basic understanding of these three realms. More detailed observations will be given of how ancestors and spirits from these different realms can influence people living on earth.

Article 6

The information I will describe in this special realm is like no other spirit realm I have visited. It is the highest level in the spirit world at this time and acts as a central hub of restoration.

Ancestors are able to reach the highest level of absolute purity which allows them to blend and harmonize individually or, as Blessed couples, directly into Gods pure heart of love.

Blessing large numbers of your ancestors can form a strong barrier that can help protect you from the chaotic and negative environment that we are all confronted with in everyday life on earth.

A question asked in one of the previous articles was: "Is it possible that my wife can join me so we can live together in the spirit world?" I will now describe this realm where you can remove any narrow-minded thinking and old traditional resentful history. This then becomes for you a total liberation of your spirit and opens the possibility of being reunited with your husband or wife. I will explain where a liberation process works and why it's important to have a good understanding of this realm as it will make it easier for you to relate to further testimonies.

In Korea, the Cheongpyeong geographical region on the earth has a parallel Cheongpyeong in the spirit world. They both work in conjunction with each other. Unification members, or indeed anyone, can attend and take part in the different liberation programs offered there. Through attending these programs at the earthly campus, you attract many of your ancestors who have also been requested to be looked for from deep within the various areas of spirit world. The 'found' ancestors gather in halls within the campus walls and wait to be guided to the spiritual Cheongpyeong campus.

Below is a picture of the earthly Cheongpyeong campus.

As you continue to attend the program, negative and resentful spirits are also released from within you. They are, in turn, also gathered together in a separate area where they are also guided to the Cheongpyeong campus in the spirit world. Those newly found ancestors make their way, guided by angels, up to the physical 'Tree of Blessing' where they then depart to the campus in the spirit world.

A spiritual experience I had when I was attending one of the programs in Korea happened when I was walking alone up the long path to the Tree of Blessing. I spiritually heard a rustling of 'spiritual wind' coming up from behind me. I turned around and could see a long line of spiritual ancestors in pairs heading in the same direction as me. They were being guided by angels on each side of the path up towards the Tree of Blessing. As I stood watching, I felt them walking right through me as they continued on their way to the Tree of Blessing. There they would gather and then continue on to the Cheongpyeong campus in the spirit world.

Spirit ancestors walking in pairs

They would then be guided through a doorway into the spiritual campus which is vastly bigger than the one on the earth. It has the same arrangement and setup as the campus on the earth.

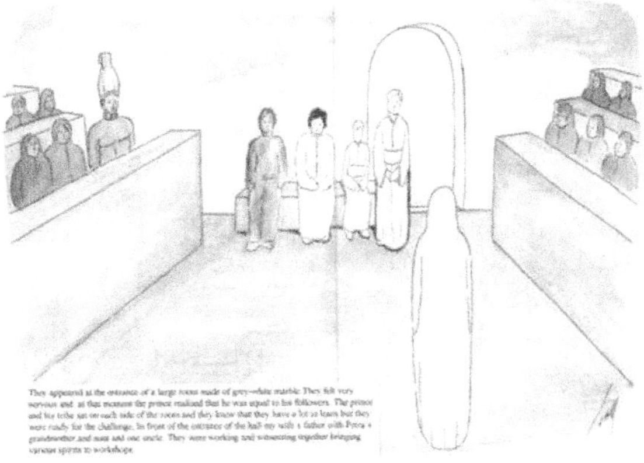

Below is a picture of the spiritual Cheongpyeong, the difference being that there is no limit to the size of the buildings.

In here they were guided to take part in different programs where they watched on large screens how history has developed and changed over the many centuries. The new truth being revealed is the Divine Principle. It is explained in great detail, describing how God has been working over the centuries to bring mankind to a complete understanding of the purpose of life.

All this happens in different rooms within the spiritual Cheongpyeong campus with lectures being taught by different members who passed away several years ago. The spiritual 'students' are supported by their own Blessed ancestors whom they have not seen before. Nevertheless, they were the ones that found them and could sense their direct relationship. This can bring comfort as they learn and develop spiritually. They also get to know their new environment along with meeting up with relatives who they've possibly never seen before, being separated in different realms for generations.

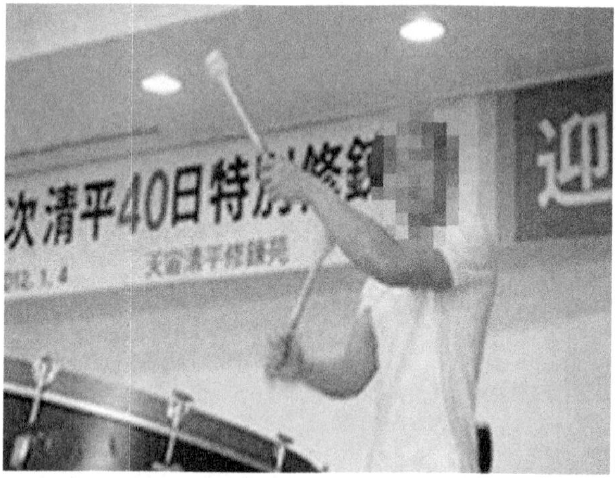

Drumming during the Liberation ceremony...

These 'spiritual students' then take part in 'Liberation' workshops to remove negative and resentful spirits which have accumulated within their own spirit over thousands of years. Ancestors that have removed all traces of their old history through the liberation program continue to reside in this realm and, having reached a level of spiritual cleanliness, they then go on to attend a Blessing ceremony.

Spiritual Blessing Ceremony

Ancestors become reunited together as couples with their love ones whom they have not seen for possibly centuries. They were separated from each other at whatever historical time or age they passed into the spirit world.

Within the traditional earthly marriage vow was the saying "till death do you part." But now, within the new liberation process, this tradition is completely removed and replaced with Gods true vision for mankind. This makes it possible for you to become reunited with your lost loved ones, enabling you both to live together in harmony in the eternal world now as a Blessed couple.

A newly discovered set of principled laws of how the spirit world operates is taught, along with a new understanding of who God is and the true reason God created mankind, based on those new principles. As negative and resentful spirits are removed, a new understanding of your own root origin from deep within you is discovered - God *is* our True Parent and root origin.

As you free yourself from the dominance of negative and resentful spirits, Gods pure love is allowed to come to the surface within your spirit, giving you an awareness of who you really are for the first time.

The discoveries of this new principled truth have opened a revolutionary door in this 21st century. As couples pass into the spirit world, they are separated and guided to a realm that is complimentary to their character and outlook on life. Here they will stay unless they are called out by one of the Blessed ancestors who will invite them back to the Cheongpyeong campus to take part in a liberation program.

As the liberation program progresses and ancestors remove all the negative and resentful history from themselves, they become absolutely good pure spirits who are then reunited with their loved ones and together attend a Blessing ceremony.

The Blessing ceremony allows the union of the once separated couple to harmonize in God's pure love and emulate God who is masculine and feminine. The Blessing and their union allows them the freedom to travel anywhere in the spirit world. This is the unique aspect of this spirit realm. There is no other place that can offer this possibility anywhere in the spirit world or physical world. Gods original plan for mankind was that, as husband and wife, you would live together along with your ancestors in total spiritual freedom. You would be able to travel anywhere in the spirit world as a couple with no restrictions or limitations for eternity.

You will be able to visit the three spirit realms described in the previous testimony from the highest to the lowest spirit realm because, having removed your negative history, no negative or resentful influences can stick to you or have any influence upon you.

This is why this special and unique realm that offers a liberation and Blessing program is absolutely vital to the restoration process. It offers the only way to educate and liberate people on the earth and to restore ancestors that have been trapped and lost for centuries in the spirit world. It can bring them back to their original status as children before God, or root origin, and True Parent.

I explained before that in order to leave your particular spirit realm and enter this realm you need to be invited by a Blessed ancestor. There is usually a 'request form' transferred from the Cheongpyeong campus in the physical world to the one in the spirit realm requesting that an ancestor or relative from a descendant living on the earth be searched for and called out from their particular spirit realm. Searching for that relative begins and, when found, they are brought back to the campus where they are offered the chance to take part in an education and liberation program.

Here on earth, Cheongpyeong stands next to a beautiful lake.

Anyone can go to attend the education and liberation programs to liberate and restore their personal ancestors. They can remove any historical negative and resentful spirit their ancestors caused others, which they unfortunately inherited. Along with this they can also remove any resentment from their own spirit that has built up through their own life experiences and struggles.

As these programs come to a conclusion, the liberation and Blessing ceremonies take place and a 'welcome home' ancestors' celebration is made to welcome all your restored Blessed couples into your home. Ancestors have a vested interest in helping their descendants to be successful, especially the children. Here the ancestors can blend into and occupy the parents and children's spirits and help bring guidance and heavenly fortune to their descendants' lives. The more Blessed ancestors you have, the more spiritually stable your family can become.

A 'welcoming home' ceremony in your home.

The influences I observed on Blessed couples and the different benefits that Blessing your ancestors can have on you, rather than leaving them single.

Your liberated ancestors can only come together as couples and return home to you after they have become Blessed, which means they can become frustrated with you if they are waiting too long for their Blessing. They are unable to do anything for you. They cannot even meet together as couples. This can only happen when they become Blessed.

Blessing the ancestors you liberated would be a suggestion since many people leave them too long before doing this for them. You spiritually pick up their frustration which can cause you to also feel tension and frustration. Blessing them will enable them to be able to return home and directly influence and support your couple and children.

Doing a 'reading' for a Blessed physical couple, I observe that they have many different ancestors helping each of them separately in each of their spirit realms. Their Blessed ancestors are couples who are totally united in God's pure love Thus, their influence is very different from that of single ancestors. When they become Blessed as husband and wife, they will return home to both of you and blend into each of your couple's spirits since you are husband and wife, just like them.

Your Blessed ancestors harmonize and unify focusing on Gods pure love as Blessed couples. They will blend into each of your physical couple's spirit which will directly help and improve your couple's relationship.

The single ancestors you have with you are active to the best of their ability and supportive in their characteristics. They also blend into your spirit since you inherited those characteristics from them from the time you were born. This allows them to support you both, in whatever way they can.

The problem for you is that those single ancestors are narrow-minded in their thinking and outlook on life. These old influences are there because they have not yet been liberated from their old traditional thinking, habits and lifestyle through the liberation and Blessing process. Many of these ancestors are from your side lineages and must wait for the Providence to open to them. When this happens, it will allow side lineages to become liberated and Blessed. At this time it is only your direct lineages that have the opportunity to become liberated and Blessed.

My observations on how single ancestors change when they become Blessed.

When they are single, they are very narrow-minded in their thinking as they have not been liberated from their old traditional lifestyle. When they become Blessed and return home to you, they will blend into your spirit and influence you differently from the old traditional lifestyle they once lived. Your ancestors' characters, who they are, and how they affect both of you will be very different when they become liberated and Blessed. They won't have the same influence on you then as they do now.

If they would have changed and purified themselves through the liberation program, their outlook on life and the character they had when they were alive would now be very different. So, the most important thing you can do is to bless the ancestors you liberated and then continue to liberate and bless as many ancestors as you can. This will benefit the spiritual and emotional stability in yourselves and in your couple's relationship.

My observations of how emotional blocks that you may experience in your couple's relationship will be removed when single ancestors are replaced by your Blessed ancestors.

Single ancestors need to be removed from you. They can then be replaced by your Blessed ancestors who are couples in love and who can completely relate to the new truth and ideal of a Blessed couple.

Your Blessed ancestors will then occupy most of your spirit, thus allowing them to influence and guide you spiritually and emotionally in your daily lives. Their influence will form the base to set both of you free from any spiritual stress or emotional conflict that you may be experiencing so that you feel more balanced and able to enjoy your couple's relationship. Having the full support from your Blessed ancestors, who themselves are 'couples in love', they will blend into each of your spirits and help you both cultivate the love in your couple that will help you both emulate and experience God's pure love.

Your relationship within your couple will naturally improve as the emotional blockage will be removed which was being caused by those single ancestors' influences. This will leave you free to express your emotions to each other more easily. To cultivate your ability to express and share love with each other as a couple should be your main focus in order to connect to the truth of this New Age. As you reach your 'twilight years', this will also prepare your couple to be able to live and blend together for eternity in God's realm, together with all the Blessed ancestors.

Having no Blessed ancestors at all is a real problem since there is no providential principled support that can blend into your spirit and influence you to live differently. Having only single ancestors can prevent you from developing a higher level of principled consciousness and understanding of the time we are now living in. This is because they can only support you the same way they have been doing for many years. They are unable to support you or help bring you onto a higher level as they have not experienced it themselves. They cannot support any new spiritual concept, vision or dimension until they become liberated from their old ideas and traditions.

There was instruction given to liberate and bless a certain number of your ancestors before a special time in history which has since come to pass. That historical time is called Foundation Day. To have achieved this, and having then gained the support from your now-Blessed ancestors, this would act as strong spiritual protection around individuals or couples. This would be most important as we enter into the 'Growth Stage', which is the next stage after the 'Foundation Stage', which has been completed.

The different programs take place regularly. If you have an interest, then take part in one of the programs. Or, if you want to know more, please contact the author.

In the next two articles I will explain how the liberation process works by describing my observations of my wife's progress as she removed her old history and the root of the negative resentments she inherited from her ancestors, plus those of her own making.

I observed this happening a few days after she passed into the spirit world several years ago. I could also observe one of the 100-day programs she was able to take part in.

Article 7

A Testimony of my observations of my wife Petra's 100-day liberation program that took place in the spirit world.

Part 1.

Being able to see into the spirit world, I was able to observe the changes taking place in someone (in this case, Petra) going through a liberation process in the 'spiritual Cheongpyeong' in order to remove her negative and resentful historical problems inherited from her ancestry.

After attending this process, you are set free spiritually and able to move and travel anywhere in the spirit world with no restrictions. You are able to visit any spirit realm and not become trapped there. This is what the liberation process offers to anyone who applies for it.

If you would like to apply for this liberation program on earth, please contact the author.

My wife Petra passed away on the 30th of January, 2015. She has been appearing to me in spirit ever since then. Later, on the same day that she passed away, I met up with my daughter Christabel at the hospital where Petra was taken. We went to the morgue to view the body, which is where I saw her spirit for the first time.

Her body was lying on the table on her back, and looking very peaceful. At the end of the room, about two meters away from the body, I could see her in spirit standing between her father and mother. They had also passed into the spirit world a few years before. Her parents were there to greet and welcome her into the spirit world and to her new home.

Petra looked very bright but a little dazed, still wondering where she was. Soon she was able to grasp what had happened. She looked much younger; I would reckon her age to be around 21 years old. She also looked slim and sporty with her hair pulled back into a ponytail. Her hair was a golden color, just as it was so many years ago when I first met her at the matching time. Her parents radiated a bright white color that made the room brighter.

The white energy coming from her parents was their own spiritual energy radiating to the surface of their bodies. It covered the whole surface of their spirit bodies, appearing as if they were wearing holy white gowns.

Their energy was pure white, whereas Petra's spirit and energy appeared to be bright gold. This was possibly because she had been liberated a few months before her passing, which is one thing you can do now in Cheongpyeong. You can be liberated before you pass into the spirit world in order not to be in limbo until someone liberates you. She could therefore step out of her physical body directly into a higher realm.

Petra was taken to the 100-day spirit workshop program where you learn to live and think as a spirit. The spirit world is so very different from this physical world.

One example is that other spirits can hear what you think, so you need to know how to control your thoughts. There is no need for sleep or to eat food, so life there is very different and needs to be adjusted to. Spirits are, of course, people without a physical body. You get to know everyone, but to do this you do not need to say anything with your mouth. You immediately 'hear' what the other spirit person says and you can respond just as quickly.

You can know very much about a person within a split second of meeting them. The spirit world is multi-dimensional, so everything is immediate. This is something we would all need to get used to in order to live in such a way. These are a few of many things that are taught in the 100-day liberation program, along with all the Principle education.

Petra has appeared many times in my physical home. I would prepare her a small meal at the same time I had mine. She would join me and we would sit quietly and eat together. She did ask me not to ask her too many questions at that time since she was also learning about everything there herself. She could not give me clear answers to many of my questions so I only asked how she was getting on.

She answered that she feels incredibly free together with such wonderful relatives and like-minded people. Petra would join me for lunch. It would consist of a drink, a main meal and something sweet for dessert. She could eat and even drink by reaching down to her glass and putting her spiritual hand around it. As she lifted her hand, the glass would appear in her hand in a spiritual form. She continued to lift the glass to her mouth and drink and at that point, just where the liquid began to flow into her mouth, it vanished.

The same experience happened when she was eating the food by using a knife and fork. She picked up the food using the fork that appeared in her hand, the same way as the glass did. She lifted the food to her mouth and at the point of entering her mouth it would vanish because Petra knew the taste of that food, having tasted it before.

Having experienced eating and drinking, she knew the different tastes. But, this eating and drinking is more of a comforting experience, helping Petra to settle into the spirit world. She did not really need the food in reality, but it was a way of coming and socializing with me.

The author of the *Divine Principle*, our True Parent, explained that we should all experience as many things as possible, be it food or visiting places, etc., before we go to the spirit world so as to be able to continue to experience those things there also.

Petra and I would continue to talk for a while and then she would slowly begin to vanish and continue with her 100-day program activity after saying goodbye.

The picture we used for the Seonghwa or ascension ceremony was a recent picture of her. I hung this picture on my wall, next to my altar. Many times I have sat looking at that picture and have been spiritually drawn into it. Then I could see Petra in the clapping sessions which are part of the liberation program, hitting her spiritual body and sometimes being helped by her Blessed ancestors, or by several bright colored angels who help support the program.

At times, she was alone depending on what was being removed from her spirit. The spirits that caused her physical sickness and brought her into the spirit world were all coming to the surface by being brought out of her through the clapping and the methodical beating of a drum sounding in the background.

The trapped resentful spirits were being coaxed out of the body. I saw her clapping and hitting herself and, as she did this, a black tar-like substance would ooze out of her spirit like sweat. It looked like it was seeping through the pores of her spiritual body, making her look as though she had been covered all over in thick black oil. This oil would run to the floor, causing large puddles around where she was kneeling. It would also be dripping off her nose like sweat after doing sports.

As I was looking at her doing this, I could see the black oily substance beginning to move. Several black lumps began to rise up out of the puddle of oil and form into the shape of people who were totally black. These black figures were then guided to the front of the hall by several bright angels that were standing around the hall, supporting the program. They would walk toward the black figures and begin to guide them to the front of the hall, where they would sign up for a 100-day workshop program themselves, in a different part of the Cheongpyeong spirit world campus, away from where Petra was.

As I continued to look at Petra, I could see that all that black oil was resentful spirits caused by her ancestors, which was what she was burdened with and which eventually caused her to go to the spirit world so early in her life. Petra knew that she was chosen by God to carry those resentments and now, through the program, she was able to remove them permanently.

Normally you would visit Cheongpyeong and attend the clapping sessions freely, but Petra being so sick could not travel, as with so many other people in the same situation. Here Petra looked older during the clapping sessions. However, Petra knew that she could remove those sins permanently through the spiritual liberation program.

It is interesting to see that even though Petra had been liberated, it only put her in a higher realm but it did not remove those sins and resentments she inherited, or made herself. This she still needed to do, but because there is a special place to do this she felt so wonderful and secure to do it.

As I looked at her, I could see her eyes closed as she was concentrating, then suddenly her eyes opened and looked directly at me. Even though she looked completely exhausted, she began to smile at me. She also spoke, saying that it was so wonderful to be able to remove the entire burden she was carrying for so many years. As she spoke those words, tears appeared in her eyes. Spiritually, as her tears flowed down her cheeks, it washed away the black sticky oil revealing her golden young spirit that lay beneath. She knew that she had a different inner spirit. It just needed to be revealed and she could see that when she visited me. Even though at that time she was so dirty looking, she knew it would only last a short time. Then all the rubbish and hell would be gone. Her spirit and image looked the age that she was when she died – fifty-eight. When she visits my home, her spirit appears many years younger being around the age of twenty-one, I am sure this young spirit is her true self as she can only remove the dark resentful spirits from her old spirit self.

During the following days, I could often visit her in the liberation program. I could see her 'young' spirit becoming more and more revealed. When she visited me, she would leave her old oily resentful spirits behind and over time her spirit became brighter and brighter through the program sessions. Cheongpyeong is the only place where the black oil is revealed and is a most protected place, surrounded by angels. Only there does this happen.

Over time, several thousand spirits appeared and left her spirit body and were guided to take part in their own liberation. There they will be educated and attend the clapping sessions for them to remove all the resentments and internal historical resentful spirits they themselves have been influenced by throughout their own lives. They will clean themselves up and become absolutely good spirits themselves. Then they can be reunited with their loved ones who they were also separated from and then attend a Blessing ceremony. This is why there are so many Blessed ancestors' spirits in the spirit world; not just our own ancestors. To be able to connect to your spouse in the spirit world can only be achieved through heart and love, which is the energy that blends your two spirits' together.

If there was no love connecting you together here on earth, then there will be no love to bridge the two worlds. You will find it very difficult to connect together as a couple, which reflects the relationship you had on earth.

When you dwell in the memories of love you had together as a couple, you connect directly to God's pure love. By doing that, you will naturally attract your partner to you, as I do with Petra. You can feel your love becoming stronger and more alive as God is also attracted to your memory of love. So, the spirit of your spouse enters your spirit, or visa-versa, and you become 'one' at that point, blending both spirits through your harmony of love.

This means that when I pass into the spirit world, our spirits should naturally be attracted to each other as they are now. It would feel as though I was never parted from her. If you have love, there is no boundary, even between the physical and spirit world; there is no separation. The need to develop your relationship on earth is the key, which is why we are born on earth and why the Blessing is so important.

Without the Blessing you will have no eternal partner to share and be together with to experience life eternally, and God will have no couple to dwell in and experience love through. When it becomes my time to go to the spirit world, I will also attend the liberation program there in order to remove my dark oily resentful spirits caused by the bad deeds of my ancestors I inherited from them, plus my own burdens of resentment I caused myself from my own bad actions.

In some ways I am looking forward to doing it, as I know I will free the resentful spirits trapped in me. I can become an absolutely good spirit myself, which will bring me onto the same level to be able to blend with Petra, 100%.

On the earth Petra and I could never blend easily together; only to a certain extent as she was always so sick. I also couldn't express myself to her so much because of all my own difficulties. We loved each other as much as we could, which made a good base to begin. I feel life can only get better. How wonderful is that!

Petra has met up with several of our relatives, in between the breaks of the 100-day spiritual liberation program. She will continue casually meeting up with all our relatives and getting to know them and their own histories. She is very excited to meet them all.

Petra's 100-day liberation program finished on the 9th of May, 2015. I will put on a 'welcome home ceremony' to celebrate her homecoming in my apartment. She won't just stay here with me, as it is very quiet here but she will be free to come and go as she pleases, being able to travel anywhere in the spirit world. This concludes part 1.

Article 8

Continuing the testimony of my observations of my wife Petra's 100-day Liberation workshop program

Part 2.

As time continued to pass during her 100-day program, I would sit and often gaze at her photo on my wall above a small shelf I have; her smiling face looking back at mine. At that point many times she spoke to me, asking me how my day was going and what I was doing. When she asked those questions, her mouth (in the photograph) did not move. I just knew she was asking me that, so I immediately responded saying what I had been doing and the concerns I had.

Then I would ask Petra if she had finished the liberation program and she would say, "Nearly." At that point, I was taken spiritually into her realm and into a large room or hall where she was attending the program. It was quite empty with only a few angels and people there. The room also looked quite dark, as if only partially lit. At the front of the room there was a stage. On the stage was a large table and to one side was a huge opening.

Having been ejected from Petra's body, dark black resentful spirits would then go to the front of the room where an angel was pointing to the place on a table where a new liberation form was waiting. They are shown where they should sign, or place their mark, in order to begin the their own 100-day workshop. They then leave the hall via this huge door-shaped opening, as I mentioned.

I watched as Petra continued her session. But as time passed, less and less of the black tar-like substance oozed out from her pores and eventually no more came through. As the 100-day program began to draw to an end, with only a few days left, she would suddenly appear in our living room sitting on the chair beside me. "Oh hi!" I would say, "Wow you look good!" She looked slim and sporty, as she always did when she visited me.

I was attracted to look down to her feet where I could see running shoes sticking out from under her holy gown. "Oh I never saw those before," I said. "Yes, it's quite active here," she replied. "So you're quite busy, then? Does that mean you finished your sessions?" "Yes," she said, giving a big sigh of relief.

"They were really long sessions. I'm glad I could get rid of everything. How do you know all those resentful spirits have left you?" I asked.
"I just know," she said. When I looked back through her picture at the hall where Petra did her clapping sessions, it was no longer subdued but was now all sunny and bright. All the doors and windows were open.

Suddenly I was taken together with Petra from the large room and we went outside to meet her parents and mine. They were all sitting outside the coffee and cake shop, down the slope where the pagoda monument stands and where all the tables and chairs are. "Oh, hi Phil," my mother burst out.
"Grab a seat my lad," my father said. "It's been a while," he added; "Yes," I responded. "You all look so young and fit." "Yes, we feel

great," my mother said.

At that point, Petra came back from the shop with two large strawberry drinks with straws for both of us. I think they were Yakult-type drinks. "Wow, great! They look so tall." I greeted Petra's father and mother, who just sat there grinning with joy and surprise at seeing me. They both greeted me in English, although I never saw their mouths move. I just heard what they said.

Around us were so many Blessed couples; some I even knew plus some single members. Many were holding hands or walking arm-in-arm so harmoniously, which was wonderful to see. I even saw children running and playing together. It felt just like I was at an 'annual gathering,' not a liberation program.

The sun was shining and there was a bright blue sky and a slight breeze. The surrounding slopes of trees and grass looked so green. Looking around, I could immediately see that the spiritual Cheongpyeong campus was vastly larger in size than the one I was used to back on the earthly plain. The area were we sat was absolutely huge, and the pagoda was an incredible size almost looking like a huge monument.

Amazing! The tree of Blessing also towered over us up on the hillside.

The large room where the liberation sessions take place looked so far away. Everything was so large and spread out. I could see why as there were so many more Blessed couples, plus other Blessed couples and single spirits. They were restored resentful spirits who had left their ancestors bodies or member's bodies on earth and cleaned themselves up through their own liberation sessions. All looking brilliantly white as if in holy gowns, although in reality they were not wearing holy gowns. Instead, it was God's bright pure internal energy radiating out from within the ancestor's spirit and overlapping the edge of their spirit, making it appear as if a holy gown was being worn.

They were all reunited with their loved ones which was really wonderful to see. As I looked around at every one, I knew the difference between who was related to me and who was a restored resentful spirit, even though I never met any of my own ancestors beyond my grandparent's time. I still instinctively knew who my ancestors were and they also knew me. This was incredible as there were so many of them.

I would say to some standing close by, "Hi. I'm Philip," and they'd reply, "Yes, we know." How wonderful to meet Ray and Cath's son. Just by looking once at them, I seemed to know everything about them, plus they knew all about me. This meant that we automatically felt at home with each other and without a shred of nervousness.

“So what’s Petra going to do now as she will finish her 100-day workshop in a few days’ time?” I asked. “Well, whatever she wants to do,” my mother said. “So what do you all do then?” I continued. “Well, we sometimes sit and enjoy the day as we are doing now, or we go out searching for lost relatives whose descendants want to liberate and be Blessed by inviting them to the different programs here at the campus.”

I was told of one of several ways that happens. They all go on-board a super huge ship that looks a bit like the QE2, but is a lot longer and bigger.

My mother explains that the ship leaves it’s mooring at the lake side and we all slowly head off into the dark into what seems like a bottomless realm. Each of us has a list of names we call out and hope for the right person to respond and call back. A voice could be heard saying, “That’s me.” At that point, the found person would appear on board looking, I must say, very sad and dirty and even sometimes looking wet in appearance. But of course they then begin to cheer up, knowing they have left their particular realm. They are curious to know who was asking for them.

We would tell them the name of the decedent requesting to find them, which they immediately recognized, and tears would fill their eyes with absolute relief at being found. We would sit them down on a chair and throw a blanket around their shoulders. Wanting to offer them a hot drink, we would ask what they preferred. As they named it, the hot drink would appear in a cup. This certainly made life a lot easier as they all came from different times in history and most had never heard of tea or coffee. But, God knew what they needed and would supply them with it.

“Funny enough,” my mother continued by saying, “the drink never got cold. It also never became empty, no matter how much was drunk.” What still amazed my mother was that the first question many of the found ancestors asked was if we saw their husbands, wives or parents on these journeys, with some even asking about their children. They never really knew they would be separated when they entered the spirit world. They recited their marriage vows agreeing on 'til death do us part' but never really thought about what it really meant. They never experienced the spirit world before and so never knew what would really happen to them.

We would say to them that now you have been found. "We are sure your spouse has also been found as you are going to eventually meet with them and be reunited soon through a Blessing." Many were relieved but at the same time quite worried. We told them to have patience because their own descendants will now look after them and soon they will all be together. We continue by telling them that over time they can go themselves to search for their own parents and children, but for now just relax and be happy they've been found.

Usually at that point, the person breaks down in absolute relief. What seemed like forever being in an often dark bottomless realm of lost ancestors and spirits now felt like absolute heaven to them being free.

A bell sounds out and the ship begins to head slowly back towards the intensely bright spirit realm of the vast Cheongpyeong campus. Here, the ship comes to rest at its dock and the newly-found ancestors are slowly guided off the ship by those many Blessed members. They are then greeted by Heung Jin Nim and Damonim

together with many workshop staff, welcoming them all with huge smiles of welcome. These newly-found ancestors are then grouped together, guided into different buildings depending on the period of history they each came from. This makes it easier for individuals in each historical group to relate with one other.

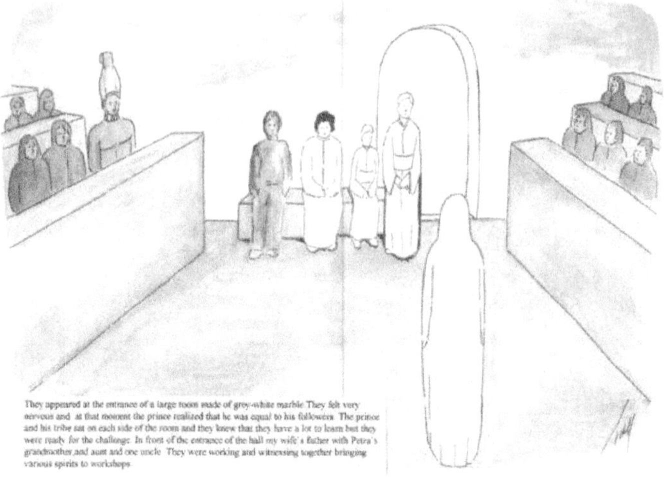
They appeared at the entrance of a large room made of grey-white marble They felt very nervous and at that moment the prince realized that he was equal to his followers The prince and his tribe sat on each side of the room and they knew that they have a lot to learn but they were ready for the challenge In front of the entrance of the hall my wife's father with Petra's grandmother and aunt and one uncle They were working and witnessing together bringing various spirits to workshops

Here they begin their liberation program with an introductory talk about why they were brought there and what will happen to them. There are many 'question-and-answer' sessions before the program begins to make sure everyone knows what is going on and why they are there and what is expected of them.

After getting themselves cleaned up through the 100-day liberation sessions, they will then go to a different 40-day session to understand about the meaning of the Blessing. Then, when that's completed, they will go to a waiting room ready to be 'Blessed' when the time is right. Now if the descendants on earth have problems paying for their ancestor's Blessing, then those ancestors will be stuck in this huge waiting room which often has large numbers of frustrated, and what seems like forgotten, ancestors

All just sat there waiting endlessly for one of their descendants to pay the Blessing fee. This becomes a big problem. At that moment; cries of joy and relief ring out as I see the door open and several ancestors are pointed out and asked to follow and take part in a Blessing ceremony. Their descendants on earth found the money to allow them to attend the ceremony.

As their ancestors guide the couples to the Blessing ceremony, you can feel the atmosphere of absolute elation from within those ancestor's hearts of love bursting out. I could see many of them looking towards those that were once their spouse many generations ago. They had been separated and lost from each other for some hundreds of generations of time. You could feel that they wanted to hug each other immediately, but they still needed a little

more patience knowing that soon they would be together forever. Those ancestors have all reached the same level of heart through the liberation program and sessions, enabling them to come from such extremely different spiritual levels to now the same level where they could attend their Blessing. Having reached the same understanding of God being their original True Parent and their root origin, and together with the universal value of heart and family values, they continued on.

I am told by my parents that God, in order to make things work smoothly, needs to use his absolute laws of restoration so that no negative influences can take advantage of anyone. This can allow harmony to reign and absolute freedom to be felt within God's realm of Cheong Il Guk, which is, of course, the realm we are relaxing in.

"Well I see," I said. "So that is what you will probably be doing then." "Yes," Petra said. "Maybe I will have a look at what I can do to support members who are trying to work with government figures here in this realm to try and have an influence on those in the physical realm on earth. The witnessing being done here can feel endless, but it is nevertheless constructive. I can also help support prayer conditions that members on earth are doing to help guide guests to workshops or special events. So many exact conditions need to be fulfilled in order to connect both worlds. I will see what I can do to help support that."

She went on to say along with all the rest of my relatives that the world is literally our oyster.

.

I then felt that my visiting time was coming to an end and I said to them, "I'd better leave you all now and look forward to seeing you all again soon."

At that point I said my farewells and kissed Petra. As I told her I will visit soon, the spiritual campus faded slowly and I was back in my arm chair in my living room, in front of Petra's picture which, of course, I had never really left. It had all happened in spirit form.

Later that morning Petra re-appeared in our living room, sitting in her chair. She said, "I will be having my welcome home ceremony tomorrow. Don't forget!" "Oh yes," I said, thinking that I had better get something prepared quickly. "Okay," I said confidently.

Petra knew something was up as I'm not usually that confident. "See you later," she said. "Okay?"

The day of the 9th of May arrived and I quickly went to buy sushi and strawberries, plus a single jam doughnut. I knew that Petra liked these, including a full, fat coke with sugar and a freshly pressed orange juice. I knew she did not need to worry about her weight anymore. I made a small 'Welcome Home' poster and celebration because actually True Mother was talking in Vienna on this very same day and I knew that Petra would be going to support that event. However, Petra did appear and was so surprised and excited at all the thought and preparation that went into her

celebration poster and table.
She happily sat with me at the table and we prayed together and then I kissed her on the cheek and said, "Please eat."
"Yes. How wonderful it all is. I won't stay long though," she said, "as there needs to be as much support as we can all give for this event. So, I will be off soon but don't worry when you go to
the event on Saturday. I remember you saying that we will all go for a German meal after the event." "Yes," I said. "That's what's planned and we will all be there together." "Okay, I'd better be off!" and suddenly she vanished. She did return later that same day and stayed for a while.
She spoke about the future, saying that she wouldn't be staying with me very much as she wanted to do so many things which she could never do when she was so sick on earth. "Yes," I said. "I really do understand that." "Please feel free to do whatever you feel called to do and we will see each other when it happens." "Good," she said with a big grin.
As we were both grinning at each other our eyes met, and as we gazed in to each other's eyes, we leaned forward and gave each other a big hug. Then she kissed me on the cheek and said, "Thank you for everything." Suddenly she vanished!
Well, I thought, that went well.
She has continued to visit regularly, staying a short while to ask me how I am and to share with me what she has been doing. I think

this is how it will be until I leave this physical world and go to join her there in the spirit world. But, I suspect even when we are together, her life won't change that much as life is too exciting for her there, which all sounds good to me.

The End….. Well, no not really as Petra will be visiting again tomorrow. Written by her loving husband, Philip.

Part Two

Readings of how ancestors and different kinds of spirits can have an influence on each one of us and what can be done about it.

- Testimony 1

  In the following testimony, a husband and wife couple asked me to respond to their questions through a Spiritual Reading.

- Testimony 2

  Questions asked as to any spiritual reason why their second son was struggling so much.

- Testimony 3

  Why a particular couple has had difficulty conceiving.

- Testimony 4

  Why has one of the children of a couple become open spiritually and is being tormented.

- Testimony 5

  Why a woman's other sister has been struggling spiritually; those influences on her sister have been intense over many years.

- Testimony 6

  How ancestors own negative experiences can cause resentment that can have devastating influences on their descendants.

- <u>**Testimony 7**</u>

  A description of a couple's spirit level, plus a description of a few of their ancestors that have been guiding them through the years.

- <u>**Testimony 8**</u>

  Addressing a couple wanting to improve their relationship, I will describe a few of the ancestors that have been guiding them throughout their lives.

- <u>**Testimony 9**</u>

  Exploring the root of some illnesses within a family.

- <u>**Testimony 10**</u>

  A spiritual reading to reveal what is happening in a person's spirit realm.

Testimony – Reading 1

As I am able to observe the spirit world, I am often asked by individuals and couples to describe what is happening to them spiritually. I do this by providing them with Spiritual Readings of my observations along with assessments of their situations.

This series of articles is of real-life testimonies of such readings. Names and dates have been removed for confidentiality.

In the following testimony, a husband and wife couple asked me to respond to their questions through a Spiritual Reading. They said their basic problem was that although the husband felt a sense of protection and guidance, the wife felt constantly insecure and spiritually influenced in negative ways that caused her physical and mental difficulties. To help explain what is going on and to reveal the root of the problem, I will describe what I observed spiritually to each of them. Then I will offer suggestions to help bring spiritual balance to their lives and improve their relationship.

To answer your questions, I entered the spirit realms of your wife and yourself through the photographs you provided. I will describe what I see which will help answer your questions.

I will explain your reading together as a couple as it will make it easier for me to describe why things are happening to your wife and to your couple. The answers to your questions relate to both of you, which is why I will present it as a 'couple reading.'

As I enter each of your spirit realms I see how ancestors and spirits are affecting both of you individually in different ways. I will describe what I see in each of your realms, and then explain how each of you are being affected by ancestors and spirits.

Husband

Entering your spirit realm, I am confronted by your spirit body that I observe is surrounded by many Blessed ancestors. They are tightly packed around you and generate a bright energy.

On the outside of this group of Blessed ancestors are many dark negative spirits that want to get close to you to in order to enter and occupy your spirit and have an influence on you. But, they are blocked out by the presence of the Blessed ancestors that are tightly packed around you. This is what I see happening in your spirit realm. I will go on to explain more later on.

Wife

When I enter your spirit realm, things look quite different. Your spirit body is surrounded by many dark spirit people. Very few Blessed ancestors occupy your spirit.

These dark spirits enter and occupy your spirit body on a constant basis. They absorb a percentage of your vitality elements and cause different problems in your physical body by draining its vitality elements, which is the basis for many of the problems you described to me.

Being drained of vitality elements makes your body feel heavy. This can put pressure on your heart, stomach, circulation and blood flow which can manifest as physical problems. In turn, this can affect your organs and make you feel psychologically off-balance, which can lead to mood swings. Your desire to control things at home is an attempt at stability to counter this.

Blessed ancestors that occupy your spirit, being very few, struggle to prevent those negative spirits from entering and occupying your spirit and draining your energy, which of course is the reason you struggle so much.

Looking back through your ancestry, I see that many of your ancestors followed a religious lifestyle as monks and nuns. Also a large number had held servant positions in large houses, which was a respected profession back then. I also see teachers, boat builders and many others who are all good-hearted people. Many of these are now 'Blessed' ancestors.

Your religiously-minded ancestors had a freer outlook on life and were guided to marry and have children in order to keep the lineage going and to pass on their devotion to descendants. They were guiding you to meet the Messiah.

Many of your ancestors originated from large families that met frequently, along with many other uncles, aunts, and other close relatives. They enjoyed socializing and supporting one another.

Husband

As I look at your photograph I am taken back through your history and shown ancestors that were very proud and vertical in their outlook on life. I see many good-hearted ancestors; several priests, monks and nuns who married later in life in order to preserve the lineage. These are now 'Blessed'.

They guided you to meet the Messiah.

Many of these ancestors surround you and continue to bolster the vertical attitude and outlook they passed on to you.

What you inherited from your ancestors was their devotion towards Heaven and the Messianic providence. When those ancestors were alive, they practiced devotion and sacrifice which formed a base for God to be able to work with them and guide you to meet the Messiah in the special time in history that we are now living in.

The problem is that although you inherited devotion and a God-centered attitude from them, which you maintained throughout your life, you are still thinking and behaving as a single person does, even though you now have a wife.

The ancestors that passed on to you that single-attitude outlook are now 'Blessed' and have transitioned into couple's relationships.

Yet *your* thinking has not elevated. The purpose of the Blessing is to emulate God, who is masculine and feminine, and to connect directly to the Creator through the love you have for one another as a couple.

The Blessing is about couple's relationships that emulate God in this physical world so as to bring Heaven down to the earth. Restoration in this time is about moving from the single to the couple ideal, allowing each of us to connect to God, our True Parent, as a united couple.

Although you inherited those single qualities which protected you all your life, now you have to move beyond the single outlook and into the ideal of the couple.

Having a strong vertical outlook on life has attracted to you those many Blessed ancestors who come to support you. Having many Blessed ancestors tightly surrounding you prevents negative energy from entering and occupying your spirit.

The negative spirits want to create problems in you, but because they cannot easily enter your spirit, they target your wife and attack her instead.

Those negative spirits want to manipulate and find ways to divide you as a couple. They know that if they can weaken her, they can hurt you. As you are a couple, you will be affected by how she is physically and emotionally. This is the reason she is being badly hurt by negative spirits.

Wife

Your Blessed ancestors find it difficult to enter and occupy your spirit because of the presence of these negative spirits that surround you and get within your spirit body. So, the Blessed spirit people have to either stay back or work together with your husband's Blessed ancestors in order to support God's providence.

This is similar to what is happening in the illustration below.

Your couple is out of balance, with Blessed ancestors surrounding and supporting your husband while you, the wife, have very little support. I will explain why this is happening and suggest ways to correct this situation.

Husband and Wife

True father spoke about a 90° vertical-horizontal angle that needs to be created and cultivated within your couple Blessing. The inner focus of you, the husband, is on providential events because of the different responsibilities and positions you carry.

The horizontal or emotional relationship you both have as a couple is quite weak and often gets blocked. This causes you both to spiritually separate even though you live together physically. The influences and habits the husband inherited from his single ancestors are influencing him to live a single life.

Even though his ancestors are 'Blessed' and have moved on, he continues their 'single' outlook on life because he grew up under their influence which has built up momentum over the years.

His spirit body generates a lot of God's love, but this love is focused in a vertical, internal way towards Heaven and the providence, which keeps him isolated.

You, the wife, also generate a lot of God's love, which radiates from deep within you and out to the edges of your spirit and beyond. Negative spirits are attracted to that bright vitality of love and absorb a percentage of it, which is causing you different problems.

Your inner desire is to send or share love with your husband. The problem is that your husband doesn't respond so well to the love you give him and only a small percentage is absorbed into his spirit.

Husband, because you block the love your wife sends to you, she becomes frustrated. You wife endures the stress as she doesn't want to give you any problems but only wants to support you. But ironically, by doing this she attracts negative spirits that live off her bright vitality element.

You, the husband, have many providential roles to carry out. It is important work and receives spiritual support. In a pioneering situation, all would be fine. However, a single-minded attitude can be detrimental when you have a family or are part of a couple.

I see two individuals – whose spirit realms are separate – living in one home.

To correct this situation and to allow Blessed ancestors to enter and occupy your wife's spirit, you as the husband need to understand what is happening in your spirit realm.

You need to develop a different attitude and outlook on how you relate to her. Only as a couple can you both emulate God and connect to Heaven.

When your outlook changes and you understand that you need to feel much closer, your 'Blessed' ancestors will be able to harmonize and occupy her spirit. They will continue to support you but, better still, your ancestors will also blend together with the both of you. That is how it should be.

Your relationship can be bolstered with an exchange of love and care. Until now, this has not been happening much. When it does, the negative spirit people will not be able to attack your wife. They will be pushed right out of her spirit realm by the atmosphere of love, allowing your 'Blessed' ancestors to enter and occupy both your spirit realms.

As an individual, you are only half a person and have but a small amount of power to protect yourself. But a couple can generate love and together mirror God. This quality of love is far greater than individual love. It has a creative energy which a single person cannot achieve.

Uniting in love as a couple attracts God and your 'Blessed' ancestors who themselves are united in love. In that atmosphere of love, they can blend into each of your spirits and bring overall harmony to your relationship.

Even when you are not together, to share a concerned or loving conversation on a phone will create this bridge or connection. You don't need to be physically together to be united in love. Negative spirits, to have any influence over you both, need to first separate you and make you both focus on yourselves.

You can combat this by focusing on your couple's relationship and cultivating the love you have for one another. When you do this, God and your Blessed ancestors will immediately enter and occupy each of your spirit realms. Over time your realms will blend into one.

Your wife may feel that there is no center of authority in your couple. She sees this as a weakness, which may be the reason you feel she is over-controlling at home. It could also be why she is struggling to stop an increasing weight problem. Furthermore, the emotional, physical and spiritual stress she feels may be putting pressure on her heart and stomach.

The challenge, of course, will be to calmly share this reading together.

I hope that you can both understand what is happening within each of your spirit realms and the effect it is having on your relationship. I hope that it becomes clear to you that the purpose of your Blessing is to blend together in love which can happen in many different ways -- taking time to cultivate a genuine interest in each other's lives, making each other happy, and living unconditionally for each other – then harmony will manifest within both your spirits and

fuse you as a couple.
Achieving a vertical connection to Heaven that focuses on the providence and connecting horizontally with each other, through selfless love, will create that ideal 90° angle which True Father often spoke about. Do you remember that he also said that there would be no shadow?
The vertical and horizontal represents your connection to Heaven and to the earth. Your couple's harmony brings Heaven and earth together, thereby completing your Blessing. That's what it's all about.

When you enter the next world you will take your spirit body and the love you cultivated as a couple. On your own you are only half a person with very limited love.
God is masculine and feminine, united into one. Masculine love is different from feminine love. But both loves blended together will create and fully express God, the source of our love. The quality of love you have as a couple, which is manifested through your spirit, is a wonderful foundation for harmony to express itself within your couple.
As you can't bring anything with you after earthly death except your spirit body and the couple-love you have cultivated, you will

need to connect to the source of creative energy that allows your desires to be realized in the next world.

So, your purpose in life is to blend in love as a couple. You will take this love with you to the spirit world. Couple-love – a manifestation of God's true love – naturally permits you to inherit and own everything you may want in the world of spirit.

God, our root origin and our True Parent, is this source of creative love. When you have experiences of couple-love, you blend into God's creative energy.

When you enter the spiritual dimension, no matter which partner goes first, you will naturally merge into that love and connect together.

That love will also link the two of you, even when one is living in the spirit world and the other is still on the earth. Love is the bridge that links. Spirit-physical separation is neither more nor less than being separated from each other by geographical location – just as husband and wife who are in two different countries.

The realm of love you blend into when entering the world of spirit, 'couple-love,' is the Cheon Il Guk realm where, along with our True Parents and Blessed ancestors, you'll dwell within the Heavenly Palace.

God, being the First Parent, wants to give you everything you desire. But he can only do this within the realm of 'true love.' Couples with little or no love in their relationship live spiritually separate lives. So when they transition to the next life, they won't go to the highest realms of love but will be guided to a realm where they can each relate as individuals until they are called out and guided by their Blessed ancestors to a liberation workshop in Cheongpyeong.

God, as our parent, wishes to give a person what they want. Consequently, the earthly attitude a person maintains will continue into the next world. So a couple who are emotionally separated on the earth will be separated from each other until they are liberated from that particular spirit realm. Consequently couples may remain separated in the spiritual dimension for many years.

Love blends the couple into oneness. This true love has to be cultivated while we are on the physical plane, as it is far more difficult to do in the next life.

Even though we all struggle to unite in love as couples, full and complete unity is possible through the liberation ceremony in the spirit world. This is achieved by dissolving the negative resentful history that each of us carries. Such is the importance and the meaning of the liberation process that each of us will go through. One could say that love in spirit world is like money on earth. On this earthly plane, if you have no money, you live a life of want. In spirit world, the more love you have within, the better the condition of your life in that world. God is the source of life and creativity energy. When you have cultivated your couple-love on earth, then as a couple you will naturally blend into God's creative life energy. When you enter the spirit world, you enter into the same creative energy level; you take that level with you. When you ask for anything in the world of spirit, God's creative love energy will allow it to appear in front of you. But without couple-love you don't connect to the source of creativity, so nothing happens. It is akin to having no money.

This is a simple example which demonstrates how life can be when you enter the spirit world. So cultivating a good, loving relationship with your partner is a worthwhile investment in preparation for your transition to the spirit world.

Cultivating love on the earth is a good example for your children. They can learn from you and inherit your good example, which they will pass down your lineal line.

We are all trying to bring a level of love into this world to solve the many problems everyone is going through. To live by the example of love as a couple is to practice the principle of unconditional love. God's pure love in your couple's relationship will be what children and others around you will be attracted to.

Love will keep your family together. This point is missing in many families. Children search for love and learn it from their parents. Children are attracted to couple or parental love and will always support them no matter what age they are or wherever they are living.

This is the difference between single masculine or feminine love; single-love on the one hand, and couple-love on the other. Negative spirit beings can attack you as an individual, no matter how much love you may have. The reason is that you are incomplete – you are only half a person. Negative spirit people, who themselves are only single spirits, can easily manipulate a single person.

A couple united in love radiates a finer, purer energy that mirrors God. Negative spirits cannot relate to couple-love. When your couple blends in love, negative spirits are repelled. When people visit your home, any negative spirits they bring with them will leave due to the pure atmosphere and energy they cannot relate to. Spiritual tension is manifested in the stomach and heart areas. Any negative tension is focused on and expressed through these areas. When a wife expresses herself to her husband and she sees that he responds well, energy will flow through her body, mind and spirit and begin a natural healing process.

When that happens, her health improves. It will be a challenge for you, as the husband. You will need to cultivate an interest in what she says and does. Over time, your heart and love for each other will grow. As we age, this area of our relationship should become a priority and our mission should take second-place. Our mission will be passed on, but couple-love is needed right now, before we depart this earth.

High-quality love is essential in order to live well in the eternal spirit world. Such a lifestyle is definitely a worthwhile investment to make.

Conclusion

It is only reasonable to conclude that love should be the focus of your couple on this earth. Blessed ancestors are couples in love. So based on the love within your couple, God – along with your Blessed ancestors – can enter and blend into each of your spirits.

The love you cultivate is the base that allows 'Blessed' ancestors to merge with your spirits. Sexual love is not the only way to cultivate love. Be interested in each other's lives. Live selflessly for one another. Ancestors can then influence and help guide your children and your future to prosperity.

The purpose of this Spiritual Reading was to search for and find the reasons why you are both struggling and to help both of you to understand your wife's physical situation.

The reading has revealed that the spiritual root of your wife's health problems involves a weakness that can be addressed by cultivating love and supporting each other selflessly. God works in mysterious ways for the purpose of helping us all develop spiritually and emotionally; your pain has led you on a quest to find answers. My observation is that the love between you needs to be cultivated and increased. Doing so will allow your 'Blessed' ancestors to freely blend with your spirit realms. This base will give them the liberty to help and support you both directly. Until now, they have been held back by the spiritual imbalance of your relationship.

To you, the wife, couple-love plus your ancestor's presence will push out the negative energy that causes you so many problems. When that happens, a different kind of support from your Blessed ancestors will manifest and your health should begin to improve.

I know that you are a couple that has been together for quite some time. It is possible that when you began your relationship, your love for each other was strong. Over time, the love can fade or get overshadowed by different responsibilities, thereby making it easier for you to settle into an individualistic way of thinking and living.

Please understand that I am looking at your challenges only from a spiritual point of view in order to help you understand what has been happening to you and why.

I hope this spiritual reading, along with my suggestions, can help you both understand each other more deeply and can assist your ongoing spiritual growth as a couple.

Testimony – Reading 2

I made this assessment for a couple who asked if there was a spiritual reason why their second son was struggling so much. Here is my reading:

I will compile my observations of the spirit world of each one of you into a single family reading, which makes it easier for me to describe why things are happening to your son as it relates to you all.

As I enter your spirit realms, I can observe how your ancestors and other spirits are affecting each of you in different ways. I will describe what I see in your spirit realms and then explain how each of you is being influenced by ancestors and spirits.

Father

Entering your spirit realm I am confronted by your spirit body which is surrounded by many Blessed ancestors. They are tightly packed around you and generate God's bright energy. Looking into your spirit body, I see bright energy radiating out from the root of your spirit to fill the whole of your spirit body. Your Blessed ancestors can blend into your bright vitality elements enabling them to support you throughout your life and help you maintain spiritual balance.

On the outside of this group of Blessed ancestors are many dark gray negative spirits. These are spirits that dwell in the general atmosphere and ones that you bring back home from your daily activities.

Because your spirit is bright and full of vitality elements, those negative spirits want to absorb it into themselves by penetrating into the bright spiritual energy that you radiate. But, they are being prevented and held back by the presence of your tightly-packed Blessed ancestors.

Mother

Entering your spirit realm, I am confronted by your spirit body which is also surrounded by many Blessed ancestors in the same way as your husband.

Looking into your spirit body, I see bright energy radiating out from the root of your spirit to fill the whole of your spirit body. Your Blessed ancestors can blend into your bright vitality elements to support you in your life and help you to remain spiritually balanced.

Beyond this group of Blessed ancestors are also many dark gray negative spirits that dwell in the general atmosphere around you, as well as others that you too brought back from your daily activities outside of home.

Because your spirit is bright and full of vitality elements, those negative spirits also try to penetrate your spirit to reach the bright spiritual energy and live off of it. They too are being blocked by your Blessed ancestors.

This is what I see taking place in both of your spirit realms.

Son

Entering your spirit realm, your spirit body is directly in front of me. Looking into the root of your spirit body, you radiate God's bright vitality elements that enter you at a point just above the navel.

This bright energy wants to flow into every corner of your spirit body. A few, but not many, Blessed ancestors occupy your spirit. I see others standing a few meters back and not able to get any closer to your spirit.

The reason they stay back is because many of the gray negative spirits that want to penetrate your parents are blocked from doing so, and they therefore look for an alternative bright source of energy. Understanding that you are open spiritually, they are drawn to you where they enter and occupy your spirit body.

As I continue to look at your spirit body, I see in your spirit a few small white areas that look empty. These areas are where high-level spirits are able to enter and occupy your spirit. But, they are also entry points for any other type of spirit, including the negative ones.

I will describe why these areas are there as well as how they affect your spirit and the influences they have on you.

You are a person who is open to the spirit world. This can be good, but it can also cause problems for you. It depends on the types of spirits that are attracted to those areas. They can be drawn to you by the way you express your personality, and you will also attract ones that dwell around your parents. You have inherited different internal qualities from your ancestors through your parents who were guided to meet the Messiah by their good-hearted religiously-minded ancestors.

As the second child in the family, you stand in an Abel position. As we understand from the Principle of Restoration, God uses the second-born Abel-positioned child to advance his Providence. Usually, the second child acts as a channel that can draw to themselves the parents' or family's problems.

Mother and Father

This is what is happening within your son's spirit. He is being used as a conduit to channel out any negativity within the rest of your family. God is using the second-born Abel-positioned child in your family to help advance his Providence. This is necessary because of the Fall.

Your son has inherited the religious-minded qualities of both your ancestors, which is their devotion and a belief in God and the spirit world. Each of you also has empty areas within your spirit bodies. The two of you have built up a level of protection over the years of practicing a 'Principled' lifestyle and by focusing on providential events. So you have benefitted by attracting high-level spirits and Blessed ancestors into you via these empty areas. This has helped both of you to block out negative spirits in the same way your ancestors, from whom you inherited good qualities, were able to do over the generations.

I will describe the activities of some of your ancestors that are now 'Blessed.'

These are the ones who guided both of you to meet the Messiah. I will also explain why those blank areas are causing your son many different problems. I will also offer suggestions to help his spiritual situation.

Looking at a few of the 'Blessed' ancestors occupying your son's spirit, I am taken back many generations to where I see several monks and nuns. These married in later life in order to continue the lineage so that they could pass their religious experiences and vision on to their descendants.

I am shown that, by their lives of devotion and solitude, they managed to remove many earthly attachments from their minds and hearts. Consequently, those years of prayer and devotion resulted in developing empty areas within their spirits.

This allowed them to become receptive to visions and revelations that could enter and occupy those areas. Through this foundation they have been able to help God and ancestors to guide you both to meet the Messiah.

Your son is being affected because he is open spiritually. The difficulty is compounded by our modern lifestyle which provides individuals with little time for isolation and devotion. Today's new truth focuses on the Blessing of couples to create new blood lineages through the children.

Son

As you inherit this area from your parents I suggest that you try to cultivate a daily life of faith. This will attract Blessed ancestors and high-level providential ideas to you which are currently around your parents. By doing so, you will feel support and guidance in your normal daily activities.

If you don't try to develop that lifestyle, you will continue to be open to the environment and chaos within our society. Any type of spirit can be attracted to these empty areas, depending on how you are thinking at the time.

This can be dangerous as they can cause emotional confusion. The atmosphere we are living in at this time often has a low moral standard, while people you associate with as you go through life can generate confusing atmospheres which your spirit will attract.

To prevent your problems from continuing, I suggest you try to lead a heavenly lifestyle and connect with the activities of our movement. These would keep your spirit stable enough for your Blessed ancestors to be attracted into your spirit and support you.

Single ancestors from your side lineages are active and supportive, too. Their characteristics are blending into yours as you inherit their good qualities. They will support you. Those singles are assisting your Blessed ancestors, who are ultimately guiding you at this time.

Depending on your thinking at any point in time, you will attract spirits into the empty areas. If you are having a positively-minded day, you will attract spirits that support your positive emotions. A day of bad thinking will attract negative spirits.

The same happens when you make a plan to achieve something. Spirits are attracted to help in your planning. But when you are interrupted, these spirits vanish and random groups of spirits come to fill that empty area in your spirit. So while you may be inspired to plan a project, at the time your mind changes, the spirits supporting your plans will abandon you. You will find yourself unable to be inspired or to continue your project.

Your over-thinking attracts spirits that prompt you to think even more. This can lead to the confusion you feel, which quickly attracts more confused spirits. In turn, you feel frustrated by not being able to fulfil any of your projects or finish anything at all.

So the propensity to attract all types of spirits is what is causing your inability to start a project, or finish something you do start, whether large or small. When you do manage to finish something, then at the end of that task you're not sure if it was good enough. This attracts doubting spirits which causes you unrest, leading to again more doubt. Having the kind of spirit body that is open to many spiritual influences and feelings is making you sometimes believe that you are not who you think you really are. Because your family has numerous Blessed and religious-minded ancestors, and the core of your spirit is inherited from your parents, you have a strong base to attract positive spirits that will increase your positive atmosphere and outlook on life. So, keep your spiritual and physical health balanced.

By living and practicing a basic Principled lifestyle, which I'm sure your parents can help you achieve, you will open a channel that allows your bright ancestors to enter and blend into your spirit.

Being the son, you need support from your Blessed and single good-hearted ancestors. You have many, but some are unable to support you right now, which is why only a few directly occupy your spirit and not enough to prevent the darker spirits from influencing you. So you need to live a lifestyle that will create the base they can relate to.

Your Blessed ancestors' vitality elements will fill the empty spaces in your spirit, which will form a base for more Blessed ancestors to enter and occupy.

The energy from deep within you will compensate for any historical inherited weakness you may have and should help your health to improve as the vitality elements will flow around your body easier.

Particularly stubborn negative spirits that are giving you physical, mental and spiritual difficulties can be removed if you are able to attend a few liberation sessions at Cheongpyeong.

Being drained of vitality elements can make your body feel heavier and place more pressure on your joints, circulation and blood flow. Over time this may affect your organs and throw your psychological state off-balance, leading to mood swings.

As well as practicing a 'Principled' lifestyle which will allow your Blessed ancestors to be attracted to you and support you much more, you should seriously consider the ideal of becoming 'matched.'

Each of us needs to express our deep heart of love to another, especially as we grow older. If this doesn't happen, the energy circulates within yourself instead of going outwards to another person. This can cause spiritual pressure in your head and attract negative spirits to live off of the bright energy you generate. This, in turn, can attract more negative spirits and energize a vicious cycle.

An exchange of love and care needs to take place in your life, which is not happening at this time. When it does happen, the negative spirits that occupy you will not be able to stay.

Negative spirits will be pushed out of your spirit realm by the atmosphere of love you will generate as a couple allowing your Blessed ancestors – who are themselves couples in love – to naturally enter and occupy your spirit.

As an individual you are only half a person and have just a small amount of power to protect yourself. But a couple that generates love emulates God. Their quality of love is different from individual love. It is a creative energy that single people do not experience.

Understand that harmonizing in love as a couple attracts God and your Blessed ancestors who themselves are united in love. In the atmosphere of love they can easily blend into each of your spirits and bring harmony to your relationship.

By focusing on couple's relationship and cultivating the love one has for another, God and your Blessed ancestors will be able to enter and occupy your spirit realms. Over time, your realms will blend into one.

This point is important, because when you are 'matched' to a potential spouse you will also become connected to that particular lineage. So you bring into your spirit another blood lineage influence that can benefit you. Over time, elements will exchange between you and the other person and attract into you all the good qualities from your potential 'match' as your Blessing progresses.

The purpose of the Blessing is to blend together in love. This can happen in many different ways, such as making each other happy, living unconditionally for each other and becoming interested in each other's lives. Doing so will develop harmony within your spirits as a couple. At this time you are a single person who is vulnerable to the negative atmospheres around you. Having a spouse to focus on directs your emotional energy outside of yourself. Doing that pushes aside negative spirits that want to occupy your spirit and keeps you focused on yourself as an individual.

This is a difference between masculine and feminine love and couple-love. Negative spirits can attack you as an individual, no matter how much love you have. The reason is that a single person is not complete – he or she is only half a person. Negative spirits attack as single spirits too, so they can easily manipulate a person who is single or behaves as a single person.

As someone who is open to spiritual influences, it is important to find stability within a couple's relationship. Here both can support each other through love and by sharing their deepest concerns about everything they are going through.

Negative spirits know they have no power over an individual when he or she has a loving partner who they can share their heart with. Negative spirits are individuals and can torment you more easily as an individual. Blessed couples, on the other hand, generate masculine and feminine energy which emulates God. This is a creative energy.

Your couple-energy will act as a protection for your spiritual openness and allow your Blessed ancestors to naturally enter and occupy you and your spouse. Their desire is to guide and support your couple to become successful in whatever you undertake. God is our root origin, our True Parent and our source of love. When you experience couple-love, you naturally blend into God's creative energy and your life becomes balanced and guided.

Please understand that I am looking only from a spiritual point of view at your situation in order to help you understand what has been happening to you and why.

My suggestions concerning 'matching' and Blessing are based on the benefits you will gain spiritually from becoming 'Blessed.' Being spiritually open and easy to manipulate means that those negative spirits will try their hardest to prevent you from becoming 'matched' and Blessed as they know that they will have to leave you. They don't want to do that.

If you decide to prepare for 'matching,' my suggestion would be to do a 7-day cold-shower condition of which the last day is on the day you meet your potential spouse. This condition will keep you spiritually clear and temporarily push out any negative spirits that want to try to prevent you from meeting a potential spouse.

This would also allow your 'Match' to see your real personality without negative interference. If you find a spouse, continue with the cold-shower condition. Over time, as you communicate and express your emotions of love and care for one another, the need for the condition will lesson and finally end as you begin to exchange vitality elements that will enter and fill up those empty spaces in your spirit.

Your focus on the Matching and Blessing will, over time, strengthen your relationship as you cultivate your love for one another. This will allow God and your Blessed ancestors to enter and occupy you both and prevent any negative spirits from continuing the problems you are experiencing as an individual at this time.

These are my suggestions, as I said before, based on the potential spiritual benefits that you could receive.

Testimony – Reading 3

A couple requests a spiritual reading to help discover why they have difficulty conceiving. I will first enter the husband's spirit realm and explain what I am able to see happening there. Then I will enter the wife's spirit realm and describe her situation. I will then summarize and suggest ways to solve the problem.

Husband

Entering your spirit realm, I can see your spirit directly in front of me. It is surrounded by many ancestors dressed in different historical costumes plus many spirits that are light-gray in color.

Above your head is a pillar of energy descending from Heaven and coming to rest on the top of your head. Through this pillar of energy, many spirits and good-hearted ancestors flow down from Heaven and enter and occupy your spirit.

They enter this way because you are surrounded by many other ancestors and spirits. These ancestors that flow down that pillar of energy are religious in nature and have a direct influence on you.

You may not be religious yourself, but those good-hearted ancestors are from a religious background and they focused on dedication and sacrifice when they were alive. You inherited their dedication and sacrifice, but not necessarily their religious aspect. Because you inherited that part of their make-up, they can easily enter and occupy your spirit and support your good outlook on life. Sacrifice and a determination to help others around you is also a character you inherited from these good-hearted ancestors. The ancestors that stand around you in your spirit realm are not so religious and many wear army uniforms of different ages.

The atmosphere around these ancestors is quite heavy and full of intense experiences, many experiencing the horrors of war. Several were killed in battles or civil unrest through many generations.

There are other ancestors standing around you. They were poverty-stricken and experienced starvation. Others, having nothing, found themselves and their families suffering the severe hardships of winter. This is how bleak the atmosphere is that surrounds you. Some of the gray spirits are of people that were tormented or killed by your ancestors. They are allowed, in accordance with spiritual law, to visit the descendants of the ancestors that persecuted them, which is why they are nearby you.

Because of this situation a channel of energy or pillar descends from heaven, allowing the religious and good-hearted positive ancestors and spirits to bypass this situation and be able to enter directly into your spirit. Their purpose in doing so is to inspire you to keep thinking in positive ways. They do this because you are not responsible for your ancestors' actions that surround you and so they want to protect you as best they can from those experiences. But because the negative presence is there, many times you pick-up those depressive, moody atmospheres that sometimes make you feel isolated or empty.

The difficulty you have in expressing yourself is due to what is around you. Nevertheless, the pillar of energy descending from Heaven is very positive and keeps you somewhat safe by forming a protective barrier.

Looking at your spirit is like looking at you within a sausage skin, very tightly wrapped. Your good-hearted ancestors want to protect you and try to prevent those spirits surrounding you from entering and occupying your spirit, so there is this tight skin around your spirit. However, the heavy atmosphere beyond that protective skin prevents you from easily expressing yourself to others.

Many of the good-hearted ancestors that enter your spirit through the pillar have religious backgrounds. There are monks and several clergy who lived many generations back. Because they are single, they influence you in a single-character way. The monks denied their sexual emotions and feelings which they saw as sinful and earthly temptations of Satan. Consequently, they spent many long hours removing these feelings through prayer and abstinence, and also fasting.

These types of spirits guiding you through your life have helped keep you focused and given you the ability to live humbly and cope with problems. Unfortunately though, they could not help you promote your emotional self or to find ways of expressing that to others.

This means that you naturally suppress your God-given emotions and sexual drive. This is part of the cause of difficulties within your relationship. Those religious-minded ancestors, who are influencing you now, were unable relate to women. You too are burdened by the same attitude. The main difference now is that we live a very different lifestyle compared to those ancestors. They were able to choose quiet lives or live within groups of like-minded people who would spend hours in prayer and devotion to find ways to suppress or remove those emotions.

Quite contrarily, you are living in our modern age among mixed genders and with free and easy access to social media and other stimulations. Although this mix of present-day experiences allows you to share with and help others socially, the problem arises when it comes to expressing your deep emotions, passions and desires. At that point, you unconsciously begin to suppress those feelings and desires.

Possibly you are unaware of this and rather feel that you are expressing such feelings. But in reality, they are blocked. This is part of the reason why your couple is unable to conceive.

I will suggest ways to help you. But first I will enter your wife's spirit realm and describe what I see happening with her.

Wife

Entering your spirit realm I see your spirit directly in front of me. It generates bright energy from deep within. This energy is flowing to the edges of your spirit body and out into your spirit realm. You generate an atmosphere of love which is supported by many ancestors that surround you – mainly women. Many are wearing period costumes and they have a happy outlook on life.

Most are married into large families and loved to socialize. Your energy flows out horizontally, giving you the ability to socialize with others and affect people in very positive ways.

But when you meet others, you often absorb a heavy atmosphere that they may be carrying so that afterwards you sometimes feel a little tired. This is because you will have taken on their heavy feelings. But fortunately, you will feel better after a short time. They, on the other hand, will feel good after leaving you because they will have absorbed lots of positive energy from you.

While you are a very social person who is able to give out to others, you also have many religious-minded ancestors who travelled to far-flung lands as missionaries. A good many were nuns who, generations back, sailed to different continents on large wooden ships. They would often travel in small groups to New World countries like Brazil and the Americas where they felt called to share the truth with the indigenous populations.

Many of your ancestors were educators who created schools and helped raise the spiritual level of the populations. But, they never personally stayed very long in one place as they felt a calling to bring the heavenly truth to yet more undiscovered tribes and groups.

After fulfilling years of missionary work, some of your ancestors felt guided by God to marry and start families of their own in order to pass on their religious traditions and experiences to future generations. Your ancestors had very strong personalities that helped them to do missions in non-chartered areas. They were brave and willing to give their lives to help spread the message of God.

These are good ancestors who helped guide you through your life and they are still supporting you now. You inherited their qualities of love and compassion plus a sense of adventure and a willingness to help others around you.

However, like your husband, you too may not be very religious as you mainly inherited from those ancestors the qualities of passion and devotion. You are not, of course, living a rigidly vertical lifestyle of faith as they did. Their time was very different from ours and we are influenced from many directions.

You also have ancestors of other backgrounds with different outlooks on life. Many were simple folk who focused on families and farms. Some were educators or governesses in large houses or at all-girls schools, and there are some from other professions, too.

I will now describe what is happening in your couple and suggest ways that may be able to help your situation.

Wife

Your ability to share your warm heart of love freely and make a good horizontal connection to others is a good and helpful quality. Your husband has a vertical connection to Heaven. The energy forms a very tight skin around his spirit which prevents him from easily expressing himself to others, as you are able to do.

The horizontal connection is where emotional love, passion and sexual drive are generated, creating life on this earth. The vertical connection with Heaven doesn't have such qualities. Prayer, devotion and sacrifice generate a different energy which is more sterile and internal. It doesn't have the qualities to generate vitality life elements as it does in the physical world. You need both vertical and horizontal attitudes to live a balanced lifestyle. The vertical outlook gives you guidance; vision and inspiration that can help guide you through life and seek out the best opportunities. The horizontal outlook develops your relationships, your emotional love, passion and creativeness with others around you. As a couple, of course, you need both. You are a good balance as your husband is the vertical one and you, the wife, are the horizontal one. Together, united, you can be rounded in character. That is how it should be.

The flow of energy between you flows in one direction, from husband to wife. You, being an expressive wife, can more easily give love to him as your personality is to naturally express love more freely. Because your husband's historical ancestral background is quite heavy emotionally – as was described before – due to his ancestors having struggled and suffered in sometimes horrific ways throughout different ages, he himself has become trapped and is unable to express himself easily.

I am describing what I see. Of course his ability to express love and emotion is there to a degree, as the time we live in gives us a greater opportunity to learn the skills of socializing at some level. But for him, deep emotions of love, passion, and desire, and the ability to blend together within your couple needs to be developed and cultivated.

I observe that while your elements of love are flowing to him, only a small amount is able to enter his heart. Yet, cultivating your couple's relationship is the key to your success.

A suggestion to help this situation is for you both to focus on the romantic side of your relationship and to cultivate a strong sexual desire for one another. I would suggest activities like having romantic candlelight dinners and other ways to make each other happy and feel very comfortable with one another will help.

Husband

You need to open up emotionally, while the wall around you needs to be removed during the time that you have a sexual relationship, in order to conceive. While sex is only a small part of the relationship, the time and preparations needed for the sexual act is the most important. Spend a lot of time in preparing and in touching each other's body to generate that arousal state, as this is what is missing.

Wife

You don't need the sexual arousal as much as your husband does, so your focus should be on him. He needs to become intensely aroused. The vitality elements generated in both of you comes directly from God.

God's own creative energy originates deep within himself. God is masculine and feminine. The energy that flows between the masculine aspect and feminine aspect generates creative energy that harmonizes into one.

Because the Creator is constantly in that state, intense love-life energy flows out from God into the creation to maintain it and keep its existence. Because God is eternal, then everything created is also eternal in one way or another.

You need, as a couple, to emulate God. That is what needs to be done. Find ways to blend together in harmony and love. When each of you stimulates each other in foreplay, your desire for each other becomes stronger. When that happens God will be attracted to your couple as he will be able to relate to that state of emotion you feel together.

At the moment your desires are not strong enough for each other. Each of you is medically fine, but the emotional and passionate vitality elements are weak.

It is said that absence makes the heart grow fonder. When people who are apart spend time thinking about each other in passionate ways, when they do eventually come together they can easily harmonize in that love and expectation.

A way to find closeness is to clean each other in the shower while spending a large amount of time just being close to and stimulating each other, but not necessarily building to a climax. Repeat this for several days, gradually building momentum until by the end of the week you can decide to make love.

The stimulation through the week not only cultivates the passion and desire for one another, but the quality of the egg and sperm is full of the love and vitality elements needed for a conception to be successful. This suggestion will balance out your ability to share love together. Vitality needs to flow freely within your couple from one to another, which will be absorbed into the eggs and sperm. I am sure that if there is enough passion for one-another, you should be able to conceive.

Wife

Another suggestion is to do a urine condition. Drink a small glass of your own urine in the morning of the days that you are stimulating each other and cultivating your passion in your relationship. This is something many do in the Orient for health reasons. The reason why this can help with conception is that you will reintroduce into your own body different hormones that can raise your hormone level, making your more prepared to receive your husband's sperm.

The effect is like homeopathy: you add a small amount of a substance and the body reacts in a strong way, in this case by raising your hormone levels.

Your husband can participate if he wishes, but it is okay if he does not want to as it's mainly a condition for you, the wife. This condition could be for a period of seven days, mainly around the time you are cultivating your emotional intensity. This will generate strong vitality elements within each of your bodies and spirit, which will attract God to enter and blend into both of you.

Combined with the urine condition, which will help improve your fertility, is a strong sense of passion, longing and desire. Doing this will increase the ability of your body's reproductive area to be more fertile, which will give you a stronger chance of becoming pregnant.

I have given this direction to several couples over the years and many, but not all, successfully conceived afterwards. Love is a creative energy. God is love and the creative source and root of our own existence. By generating and cultivating love within your couple, you connect directly with God. The build-up of passion for each other will allow God to enter each of your bodies and allow you to conceive. After all, God is the creative source and our life force, which is love itself.

The urine condition is to support and reinforce the love you feel for one another.

The difficulties you encounter in sharing love with each other are not generated by you. They are historical problems. Do not blame yourself. Most people don't know that they are affected and influenced by their ancestral background and so they remain unaware of the origin of many of their problems.

So hopefully, in seeing that the difficulties you have are historical and by following some of my suggestions, you will become free within yourself and with each other as a couple. Over time and through cultivating intimacy and closeness to each other, trust will form and develop within your couple. This should give you both the freedom to express your ideas and passion in the deepest way to each other.

Things do take time as we are living in the physical realm and are subject to the laws of growth and development. So, take your time to cultivate the love in your couple. You have to be almost craving for each other or feeling you're going to explode if you don't make love to each other. Abstain from any self-satisfaction or masturbation as doing so depletes and dissipates God's life energy. Prepare a time of abstinence such as a month where you focus on the above suggestion by keeping all the passion and cultivated love that has built up in your body and mind each day, along with the urine condition. When you do finally have intercourse near the end of that month, it should give you the biggest chance of success. Please continue to take any medications you are prescribed as it will take time to reach that kind of passionate level.

These are my spiritual findings along with suggestions from

entering each of your spirit realms to help you understand what is blocking and possibly preventing conception from taking place.
I hope that this spiritual insight can be a guide for you both to fulfil your dream of being able to conceive.

Testimony – Reading 4

A Spiritual Reading for a couple asking for help to discover the reason why one of their children has become open spiritually and is being tormented.

Very often one of our children is guided by Heaven to highlight particular problems inherited by the parents so as to allow the parents to see what is going on in their own lives. This can act as a prompt and encouragement for the parents to attend a liberation program.

Historical problems and struggles within a couple can then be tackled and restored. This is what happened through their child with this reading.

I will now enter each of your spirit realms and describe the ancestors and spirits that are with you and explain how your Blessed ancestors influence you in order to help you maintain and develop your life of faith.

I will also go back over many generations, and describe my observations of one or more major influential ancestors in order for you to get a clearer picture of why you are the way you are and what you inherited from them. This will throw light on why your child is struggling.

Husband

Looking at your photograph I entered your spirit realm. It is bright and full of many Blessed ancestors of you and your wife. They all stand united in God's love.

An intense bright energy radiates from your Blessed ancestors, similar to the floodlights of a football ground. This intense energy is God's pure love that your Blessed ancestors are focusing onto your wife, your children and yourself.

Looking into your spirit realm, I can see many different spirits standing close to you and some that even directly occupy your spirit. But many have resentful thoughts that are influencing the way you think. These spirits do not belong to your direct lineage. They are hateful and resentful spirits of people who died at the hands of a few of your ancestors.

The ancestors who caused their deaths have since received the Blessing so they are no longer affected by the resentment of those spirits. What do those negative spirits do? They are directing their hate and fury towards the descendants. At this time, that means you – and your family. I will describe the reason that so much

resentment is being focused in your direction.
Looking again at your spirit I am taken back many generations by a few of your Blessed ancestors. I observe two events in your historical lineage, both of them on your father's side. One situation happened around the 15th century at a time of violent social unrest ahead of a revolution.
A few of your male ancestors participated in the murder of several innocent people – even women and children. They did not act alone; many others were involved. But, it was a bloodbath. The people who were murdered are seething with hate and resentment in the spirit world because they were violently torn away from their loved ones and from all they knew on this earth. Any family members and friends who escaped the slaughter were left to struggle and survive without them.
Another incident broke out in the 18th century when a social disruption inflamed passions that sparked a public uprising. In the madness that took place, a number of your male ancestors joined in with others to murder many innocents by torching their bodies. Women and children were amongst the slain. These two events in your history have caused an incredible level of resentment in the world of spirit.
I am allowed to observe these events as they happen through the eyes of one of your ancestors.

I will provide a commentary now on what I witnessed:

The ancestor I have blended with is one of the people of a group surrounding a large private estate in order to prevent anyone from escaping their planned onslaught.

The attackers carry awful weapons and begin throwing fire-lit objects into the rooms of the property.

Parts of the house are ablaze. Your ancestor is looking into the window of one of the rooms. He himself is now gripped by panic as he listens to the hideous screams of men, women and children who are trapped within the fiery inferno. They shriek and scream for help until they die. The merciless flames roar on until everything is consumed.

Once the attack started, your ancestor had a change of heart but felt powerless to stop the momentum of madness. If he had gone inside the building to try to help the trapped – he thought – he would have died with them.

The dead arrived in the next world filled with hate, fear and resentment. Everything was absorbed into their spirits, which fueled their determination to exact revenge on the descendants of those ancestors.

They sought out your lineage, and their resentment and hate passed down from one generation to the next as they afflicted revenge on descendant-after-descendant. Some of those spirit people are now targeting you.

The Cheongpyeong liberation program is designed to release such spirits from their own endless pain. But, the liberation providence had not yet begun when your child was born. So, the resentful spirits began attacking your children, too.

Those ancestors who committed the crime have since received the Blessing and are beyond their influence, so the resentful spirits are now attacking you, your wife and a child. Your wife is a target because she is 'Blessed' to you and so now shares a portion of responsibility for your ancestors' lineage. But positively and more importantly, she can join with you in being able to finally stop this seemingly endless continuation of evil. I will explain how later.

When one attends a liberation program in Cheongpyeong, many resentful spirits come to the surface, allowing us to become aware of them. But sometimes we are unable to remove all resentful spirits due to their extreme stubbornness. A few put up a lot of resistance and instead resurface in another family member.

Your children can come under attack for this reason. In this case, negative resentful spirits have searched for a weak link and found it in your child. They moved into this particular child's spirit, which is not difficult for them to do as the base was inherited from you, the parent.

So, you inherited those vicious and bad spirits due to your

ancestors' evil actions.

Although you may not have seen it clearly, they have plagued you throughout your life. If it had been possible to remove them before your child's birth, then they would have been freed and 'Blessed,' too.

This situation is very sad. Please understand that the Cheongpyeong providence was still developing at the time of your child's birth. DaeMoNim had to fight extremely hard to gain spiritual insights into this unique way of creating a liberation and Blessing program. Even now, not everything has been completed and the providence is still developing.

The good-hearted ancestors who guided you to meet the Messiah have now been 'Blessed' and they are with you. Your own spirit is bright. Only the dark and resentful spirits continue to partially drain your spirit of its bright vitality elements, leaving you sometimes lacking in energy.

Many of your Blessed ancestors feel quite guilty about the problems they caused in your historical lineage. When I observe those that are close within your spirit realm, I see that many of them look ashamed and some are even hiding their faces. Why would that be so?

It is because they can still feel the emotions they experienced when committing those heinous crimes. The ancestor who watched innocents burn to death in the house feels much regret.

DaeMoNim offers, through the Great Works Azalea Festival, an opportunity to attend a "prayer-wish purification ceremony for restoration." Through this ceremony, the emotional memories of Blessed ancestors will dissipate. They will, however, still be able to recall the good and bad actions committed during their earthly lives.

As I continue looking at your spirit, I am suddenly taken back many generations by one of your ancestors to around the 16th century. I observe a male ancestor who is dressed very well. He has an important function in town and looks after the town's finances. He is well-respected.

He has had a successful marriage and a number of children. They are all good church-goers who also believe in life-after-death. The family's environment is well organized owing to their belief that 'cleanliness is next to godliness.'

This family has had a good number of prayer experiences with God and the spirit world. They believe in and feel that a time will come when a new age will emerge. This is their most deeply cherished hope and they pray for such a time to happen.

This is one of the good-hearted families that helped guide you throughout your life and brought you to meet the Messiah so that you could join in the work to build a better world for all.

Overall, the ancestral influence over you has been mixed. Sometimes you have a calm nature that feels quite balanced and organized together with a strong religious interest to fulfil God's work. But, your unhelpful ancestors sometimes plague you with feelings of guilt and torment. So, this mix of polarized influences swings you from strong emotional feelings sometimes to cool, stable, rational thinking at other times. The mix tends to destabilize your personality, which creates a problem for your wife. I will explain a little about that later.

It is important to have a good understanding of the kind of background you have in order to understand why your child is struggling so much.

Wife

Upon entering your spirit realm I am confronted by your spirit. It radiates a brilliant white color. Within your spirit stands a spirit of a young woman dressed in a white samurai fighting outfit with two short swords strapped across her back.

Her face is covered. Only her eyes show. This spirit is not an ancestor.

She was a person who supported your ancestors during times of difficulty. She was a mercenary who would be hired by villages when they came under threat.

This woman was a skilled fighter whose main aim was to protect the innocent. She was of noble background and people looked upon her as a symbol of justice, power and hope.

Your ancestors respected her highly and she has stayed on to protect your lineage. This has been her personal commitment. Your ancestors believe that she was sent by Heaven.

You and your husband's Blessed ancestors stand together in harmony. They radiate God's intense energy of love. Yet, a number of negative spirits try to get close to you and wait to quickly enter and occupy your spirit whenever you create a negative base by behaving in an unprincipled way or by saying certain negative things.

At times you do this by looking at your husband's emotional states and criticize the internal torment that he inherited from the bad deeds of his ancestors. The warrior spirit fused within you influences you to think that he is weak.

You can sense his struggle and weakness and you often fight internally to prevent yourself from wanting to reject him. But because of 'her' spiritual influence, you are seeking perfection only in individuals.

Consequently your understanding of life is vertical and is lacking the essential horizontal viewpoint. Please consider that this female warrior spirit inside you is only single. She never married, and she does not know how to behave as a woman, a wife or a mother. When you attend one of the liberation sessions in Cheongpyeong, she too will be liberated. But, at this time she remains with you. All your Blessed ancestors were once singles, of course. They now understand that true power is held in the love of a couple.

Your Blessed ancestors pray for you, but they find it difficult to blend with you totally when you focus on your husband's inherited weak points. This is because such thinking creates a barrier around yourself which blocks them out As your Blessed ancestors are couples, they can only blend and support you when you unite together as a couple. When you are divided in heart, they look at you and see two individuals living in the same house. When you remove this way of thinking, they can easily return to enter and occupy your spirit. When your couple becomes united, your Blessed ancestors will enter and occupy your spirits to help solve any problems by sharing their love with you both.

And now comes a very a serious point: In the world of spirit, love is the air we breathe. If you are unable to established and experience this love here on earth, you will not be together in the spirit world!

Your couple-love forms the bridge that unites you both here on earth and in the next world. So a marital relationship problem can also become a problem for your Blessed ancestors, who are united in love and who want to support your partnership. They chose your couple to spearhead your four different lineages.

God is our True Parent and our source of love. God is attracted to your couple through love. The main priority for both of you is to develop this pure and true love together.

In your historical lineage, your ancestors needed individual power and a pioneering spirit to fight many battles because survival was necessary. But at this time of history, the Messiah comes to earth and ushers in the new age where God – who is both male and female – can walk and live in the love you both share. There is still much restoration needed for the perfection of humankind to manifest, which is why the Cheongpyeong providence is underway.

If your husband's resentful inherited spirits did not reveal themselves through your child they would have created so many problems for your later descendants and also the struggle with your husband would seem unending.

Although it is sad that one of your children must suffer so that these problems can be revealed, it is now necessary to completely clean up the negative and resentful spirits in your lineage.

Your personality is strong enough to deal with your child's circumstances without giving up, even though your child's difficulties are very difficult and dominate a large portion of your life. Your child's situation is linked to the love within your couple.

Your Blessed ancestors can work well and be truly effective when they can blend with the love you share as a couple. A harmonious partnership will allow you to digest any negative spirits that come from your child.

Through you as a united couple, God's love and your Blessed ancestors will calm your child's problem for a while. But you, the husband, need to attend the liberation sessions to remove the base of those resentful spirits that are causing your child's difficulties. As you remove those spirits from your lineage, your child should feel more peaceful in mind and spirit. Fewer and fewer spiritual beings will be absorbed into your child's spirit over time. As the situation has existed for quite a long time, even when many of your spirits have been removed, your child will need to adjust and heal, a process of recovery that will still take a while.

Child (Western/Oriental Mix)

You, the child, have been chosen by Heaven to highlight the problems within your parents lineages, which will help the restoration and removal of those heavy resentful spirits from your family.

If left in place, they would resurface through your own children and beyond. This could continue down the lineage. So, it was important that Heaven exposed your parents' problem - through you. This is the best way they could resolve it.

It is like a double-edged sword – a good thing and a bad thing. It is good because we live in the time of the Messiah where restoration is the major issue and your family situation can finally be restored. It is bad in that you had to inherit your parents' struggles and resentful spirits.

Each spirit that dominates you has its own personality, ideals and emotions. Because each voice you hear comes from a different spirit, you don't really know who is occupying you at any one time. This has caused you to have outbursts of irrational behavior.

Each of these spirits is very selfish. They fight among themselves as to who will dominate you, and when. These are the times when you behave the most irrationally. Your mind and body cannot cope with their invasion. Your spirit is that of a beautiful Blessed child, but for now it has been saturated and covered by those egoistic and resentful spirits.

Of course you also inherited many good aspects from your father and mother's lineage, but these are sometimes overwhelmed. You also inherited a strong fighting spirit from your mother that continues to help you through these spiritual difficulties. DaeMoNim explained when you were in Cheongpyeong that the base for this was in the womb.

All inherited spiritual difficulties begin in the womb as this is the place where your personality is formed by inheriting the qualities from your parents. Any negative aspects that were passed to you can be removed through the liberation program. And within that, there is hope for everyone.

Conclusion

Your child is suffering spiritual and mental stress caused by the chaos of the father's resentful spirits, which needed to be revealed somehow so that the negative history can be completely wiped clear. This will liberate your Blessed ancestors from past wrongdoings. We are living at a special time right now when the restoration of each person's lineage can substantially and totally take place.

The spirits are trapped into causing suffering to others. They depend totally on you and your heart of sacrifice to give the Blessing to your ancestors and remove their problems. If not for your child, your problems would possibly have been ignored for years or generations.

It is a suffering path, because even though many will complete the Blessing of 210 generations, the negative and resentful spirits left by some of the ancestors' bad actions still need to be cleaned up. This can take months or even years and requires much patience. However, it is the only way.

If you, the husband, attend the liberation sessions you will remove the base of those resentful spirits. It is possible that you both have removed many thousands of resentful spirits over your previous visits, but there is more to be done, which is why they surfaced and appeared in your child.

As you continue to remove them, over time your child should become spiritually clearer and able to cope with life. Doing that should also help you to experience a smoother relationship with your wife as continuing to remove those negative spirits will allow you to express a different side of yourself.

Doing so will also remove the negative area that attracts your wife to that particular weakness in your character. She will be able to relate to you better and see a different man in her husband. (Love is like the oil within an engine that makes the parts run friction-free)

If you attend the sessions together as a couple, your wife will be able to liberate the well-intentioned but domineering female fighter, who will eventually be Blessed. This will help you to blend together with your husband much easier. It will also attract your

Blessed ancestors to stay consistently with you and not be blocked out at different times when you struggle internally. Doing all these things will help improve your child's spiritual and emotional situation. All will benefit.

My suggestion is that you both attend a liberation program to remove those problematic spirits. Also, through meditation and prayer, ask your Blessed ancestors to focus God's love upon your child, which will greatly improve the spiritual situation.

Some couples carry more historical weight than others, but the Cheongpyeong Providence gives great hope that all problems caused by our ancestors can be cleared up.

Testimony – Reading 5

One sister within a family has requested a spiritual reading to discover why her other sister has been struggling spiritually. Those influences on her sister have been intense over many years.

The sister's problems have been having a strong influence on the one asking for the reading and she would like to discover and understand the historical root of the problem in order to find a way to help her and herself.

As you are sisters, I will enter your spirit realm to search and reveal the cause that happened in your ancestry and discover why only your sister inherited the intense spiritual difficulties. But as time passes, you yourself expressed that you are beginning to feel their influence on you, also.

Looking at your photo I entered your spirit realm where your spirit is directly in front of me. In the middle of your spirit is an intense bright energy which, as it radiates out to the edges of your spirit body, is absorbed by many dark resentful spirits.

These spirits do not belong to your lineage but are spirits of people who were killed many generations ago by your ancestors. I will explain how and why they were killed later in the reading and why they are influencing your sister more than you.

I observe dark resentful spirits absorbing a large percent of your bright vitality elements. I also observe, standing a little distance behind you, your many Blessed ancestors. They look intensely bright, radiating waves of God's love. They are focusing this energy on your spirit, which is being absorbed into the bright vitality elements of the inner core of your spirit. Their aim is to support you in whatever way they can. Your Blessed ancestors find it difficult to get close to you because of the large number of dark resentful spirits which surround you. These spirits that you have been picking up from your sister have been causing your fears, anxiety and insecurities for many years. It feels like many negative spirits have been absorbed by you and are blocking you.

Your spirit is being influenced by your sister who herself carries a large number of hateful and resentful spirits who were killed by a particular ancestor you both have.

Your sister, being the second-born, is in an 'Abel' position and is being used by God as a way to speed up the Providence. She is being used by heaven as a conduit that absorbs the largest majority of the intense negative historical influences caused by your ancestors, which has freed you in order for you to meet the Messiah.

God has been separating and channeling these negative spirits through different ancestors so that you could eventually, as a representative of your good ancestors, meet the Messiah. Looking again at your spirit, I am taken back over several generations to a time of the early Christian missionaries. I will describe how one of your female ancestor's deeds has had so much influence over your sister and you indirectly.

I see a young girl about 14 years of age. She is one of your ancestors, happily doing some gardening. The sun is warm and bright and she begins to daydream. Suddenly, a voice tells her to go to the local chapel to pray. Never having been told anything like this before, she finds it surprising and runs to the chapel that was quite close to her home. She finds the place empty, kneels down and begins to pray. As she prays, Jesus appears to her. He is surrounded by an overwhelming bright white light; so bright that she cannot look at his face. But, she can feel such a warm glow of love in her heart and an incredible feeling of peace in her mind.

Jesus began to say to her, "Please help me. You are someone I can trust. I need you to become one with me. Please bring my love into the dark places where people are suffering." He continued to say, "So many people are far away from me. Don't let them stay this way." He explained that many people may die so that the young people could be freed from bad influences.

"The darkness in history should end." He encouraged her to pray and told her that he will be with her. He also told her that she will know what to do when the time comes. Jesus reassured her that she won't be alone; that he is preparing others like her. Again, he told her to "pray and to prepare yourself for that time."

This was such an overwhelming experience that lasted several minutes. The girl went home and shared everything she experienced with her parents who were simple folk and just struggling to make a living. They always felt she was chosen for something. They knew she was special and different in some way and told her to become a nun. She was so happy to get their support. Based on her experience, she joined a convent. She explained to the nuns that Jesus appeared to her and told her to prepare for a mission, and that she would not be alone. She was to bring Jesus's teachings to the dark places of the world to free the children and the younger people from their ignorant ways. Even if someone had to die, it would be better that the new spirit of truth be introduced.

She lived in quiet prayer and meditation, learning how to read and write. Her parents visited often and felt good that she had food and a roof over her head, as they could not offer her much. They felt that God was with her, which made them very proud. Time passed, and one day she was given a task to become a missionary. She would be in charge of a small group of nuns whose mission would be to go and live and witness in an unexplored part of the world. This was a dark place spiritually, but the elder nun's knew she had been prepared by Jesus for a mission such as this. She felt inspired to take on the challenge with a few others. As they set off by ship, she knew they may never return. She determined herself to help Jesus, who had so much hope and trust in her.

They travelled by ship, together with a small group of explorers, and landed on the shores of this new, unexplored part of the world. A few months later the small group of explorers left for home, leaving the missionaries there as this was the plan from the beginning. It was a hard life. Your ancestor visited many newly-discovered villages together with the other nuns, and met a lot of opposition from the village elders who rejected any form of interference from outsiders. The villagers used witchcraft that was practiced together with hallucinogenic drugs and potions. It would often possess and connect the person needing help to the dark spirits of voodoo and curses that were their age-old traditions.

It was clear that the villagers weren't going to give up easily in what they believed. The main opposition came from the tribal leaders and witch doctors. These were the dominant force within the village. The other villagers felt quite open to listen to Jesus's teachings, as the nuns were white women who could read from the

Bible. This fascinated many of the younger men who found the nuns very beautiful and captivating. The nuns also expressed much love towards everyone they met, which helped build a fondness toward the struggling nuns. The men would help them, and later the women began to respond, as well. This caused friction toward the nuns on the part of the village leaders and witch doctors because the number of new believers grew slowly over many months. This was happening because the villagers began to trust Jesus' teachings. They began to question their own beliefs and traditions which seemed very dark, in comparison.

One day the leaders had had enough of the interfering ways of the nuns and physically removed them from the village. This upset many villagers who were quite taken by the beautiful, pure character and spirit of the nuns and they began to oppose the elders. Because this happened, the nuns felt the need to offer a condition to God, to find ways to continue their mission to witness. Your ancestor, being the leader, fasted for several days and prayed intensely for many hours, being supported by the other nuns. Deep in prayer, she reflected on Jesus' words spoken to her many years before. She remembered that Jesus had told her that for many it would be better to die than live in ignorance and darkness.

She felt that this was the instruction from Jesus. And although Jesus's words were meant symbolically, not literally, she felt trapped between the goodhearted villagers and the aggressive stubborn leaders who were keeping the villagers in spiritual darkness. Through her fast she became physically weaker and contracted malaria. This began to affect her rational thinking and she would hallucinate and become very open spiritually.

One evening she became obsessed with the idea to remove the leadership from each of the villages. The other nuns knew that she had many visions and visitations from Jesus and other saints, so they felt that they could trust her ideas and visions.

She shared the words spoken to her by Jesus that people needed to die to let others out of the darkness and the nuns went along with the plan, believing it to be heavenly guidance from God. They devised a plan to drug the elders, the chiefs and the witch doctors of each village; five villages in all. With the help of positive men who supported their teachings, they would bring the witch doctors, chiefs and elders to a special place.

This place was a deep pit that was used for human sacrifices. It was a small, inactive volcano that was extremely deep, with no possibility of climbing out. One evening, with the cooperation of many men, they drugged the elders and witch doctors and brought them to this place of sacrifice. There were, altogether, about 70 men from five villages. They were lowered down into the crater and left to die. Some of the nuns could not believe they were part of such a horrific plan, and even your ancestor felt a little insecure. But, she was constantly reminded by the spirit world of her past experience that this should happen and believed it was God's heavenly guidance.

Also, still being sick with malaria, she felt driven to rid the earth of these evil elders, priests and witch doctors who kept their people in the dark. She could see a new beginning for the people where God and the heavenly traditions could take root.

So on one side, a new and better lifestyle could now be lived. But on the other side, the nuns caused huge resentment in the 70 men who were left to die of starvation in such a horrific way which is beyond description. The elders and priests cursed the nuns with so much hate as they slowly starved to death.

People who were killed by your ancestors over the centuries can go to the descendants of the ancestors that killed them to torment and persecute them. This is spiritual law and allowed by God to happen. God himself does not recognize this happening because if he did, he would be accused by Satan of creating evil. So, God has to 'look the other way' as described in the principle, but still has to allow this to happen.

The restoration history seems often strongly contradictive with different heavenly strategies being used to help mankind purge history of certain traditions and practices. This can be seen happening throughout history when cultures and lifestyles were completely wiped out through wars and diseases. God knows that people in the spirit world who died in such horrific ways will be made "new" by being liberated and Blessed in the new age we are living in. Unfortunately, and having no other alternative, and for restoration's sake, people needed to be sacrificed throughout history.

This is such a sad and horrible fact. The true value of sacrifices in the history of restoration carries heavenly consequences that only

God understands. Through the nuns deeds based on your ancestors leadership, the five villages could have a new lease of life with Christian traditions being practiced. They then became thriving communities over many years with schools being built in each of the villages. Your ancestor and some of the other nuns married and had many children. And having built their own huts together with the villagers, they could live there quite happily. They never returned home and eventually died there.

Your ancestor never totally recovered from having malaria and she would suffer over the many years of her life. This ancestor had a profound effect on her descendants (your sister and indirectly you). She passed on to her descendants a positive religious outlook on life, which is why many of your ancestors joined religious orders and became teachers of religion. All had a good and high standard, with many of your ancestors being spiritually open and able to be guided and introduced by God and Jesus to those around them as they witnessed to others. These were also the ones that guided you to meet the Messiah and are now Blessed.

The other way your ancestors are having a strong influence on their descendants is based on the horrific deed that killed many people as described above. Periodically a child would be born to one of your ancestor's families who would carry the weight of those resentful spirits from that negative history. This was necessary so that the restoration could continue to move forward. God had no choice but to channel the negative energy through a specially chosen individual within a particular family, allowing the rest of the family to be free to be influenced to follow God's direction and to meet the Messiah. If this was not allowed to happen, then there would be no progress made on God's providential history and Satan would rule everyone.

Your sister, who is struggling so much and for whom this reading is being given, is one of God's chosen individuals who is playing an important role in Gods providence. She is the one at this time who is channeling as a conduit all the resentful negative spirits into her. All these spirits have accumulated over many generations, including those that have been killed, tortured, and mistreated throughout your ancestors' history beginning with the nun and the resentment she caused. With the help of your ancestors who have received the Blessing, a complete end to the continued internal suffering and torment can happen, which will also finally bring an end to the different forms of mental illness, deformity and other diseases in your descendants.

All will benefit and become renewed through the liberation and Blessing Providence. Your feelings of insecurity and fear come from the nun ancestor who over the years realized the impact of her actions on her descendants. This also caused emotional contradiction in her, having been guided to do the deed by heaven, so she thought.

Only God really understands the restoration of her deeds. The consequence was that the resentful spirits directed the focus of their hate, anger and torment on your sister, which allowed you the freedom to directly work with the Messiah.

When your sister passes into the spirit world and can be liberated through attending the liberation program, then those negative tormenting spirits that have dominated your sister will leave her. Every time you yourself attend a liberation session, more and more resentful spirits will be liberated. Over time, you will be able to say that your lineage is cleaned up and purified with no more descendants being affected by your resentful history. This will have a good influence on your Blessed ancestors who themselves are free from any insecurity. They feel so bad and regretful having committed the bad deeds your sister is struggling with in the first place.

When the resentful spirits are removed, then your Blessed ancestors can get much closer to you and blend into your spirit, which at this moment they are struggling to do. Also, your sister will have a completely different personality and character when all the resentful spirits have been removed from her. Even in the spirit world, your sister will need to develop a new outlook on life and then will be able to ask you for forgiveness for the way you were treated by her. Having completed a liberation program, your sister will attend first a matching and then a Blessing, and together with her spouse will attend a Blessed couple program to learn how to live as a Blessed couple.

The Messiah comes to this earth to clean up the physical world and the spirit world. All will change over the years as liberation and Blessing of ancestors continues. The removal of all resentful spirits will take longer, as the negative spirit realms and spirits far outnumber the good ancestors. The liberation programs will continue long after all the ancestors are Blessed, until every lineage has no more resentful spirits.

Conclusion

You are a spiritually very strong person whose birth was prepared for years before you were born to meet and work with the Messiah. Your history has been re-living the time of your ancestor the nun who experienced, like you, being a missionary but without the bad deeds. This has enabled your 'good religious influences' to work in this new age, giving value and meaning to your ancestors' efforts of sacrifice and devotion. Your sister plays a large part in channeling the resentful spirits from dominating your spirit. But, these resentful spirits have had an indirect influence on you through the closeness you have to your sister. They have been able to pass on some of their torment from her to you.

Your sister had to carry the full weight of your shared ancestor's evil deeds. And, because of your sister's sacrifice, God could call you to help the Messiah to achieve an incredible advancement and support that was so desperately needed at this time. This allowed God to open the spiritual gates for all of mankind to enter and be renewed in this new age we are living in; a new age based on all our members' sacrifices to support our true parents through attending the liberation providence.

My suggestion to help your sister would be to attend as many of the liberation programs as possible. And if your sister could attend the sessions herself, then things would work out very differently for her, also. However, I can understand why she cannot do that at present, being 'troubled' in such a tormented way. Offering Wish Papers would help, but there are so many spirits with her that a liberation session would be more realistic as it could remove several hundred resentful spirits in one session.

Because she cannot attend herself, then please focus all your efforts on yourself in the sessions. Being sisters, you will naturally remove those resentful spirits from her, as well as from yourself. As she has been influenced by so many spirits throughout her life, it will take time to see how your influence through those liberation sessions will have an impact on her, but there is always hope for her.

This ends your reading.

Testimony – Reading 6

A spiritual reading revealing how ancestors' own negative experiences can cause resentment that can have devastating influences on their descendants.

To answer your questions concerning your family situation, I will enter both your spirit realms to discover which ancestors and spirits are influencing you both, and why.

Wife

I entered your spirit realm. Your spirit is directly in front of me and your spirit generates God's bright vitality elements. God enters your spirit just below your navel and flows out, filling your whole spirit. Your many Blessed ancestors stand close to you. Their bright light of God's love radiates from them to you and these stand close to you.

As I look at your spirit I am transported back over many generations to the 9th century, where I see one of your ancestors. This ancestor, being an elderly woman, is a grandmother of a family who own a small vineyard. She lives with her entire family which is quite large. She would often go to a chapel to pray and offer food as an offering to the spirits for a good harvest.

She spends many hours in the chapel while the rest of her family work in the vineyard. The chapel was full of pictures and saints. She wore all black and she would stand or kneel on the stone floor to pray. In her prayers she would often have visions of her ancestors who lived in Jesus' time.

She could, in her vision, see a few of her ancestors praying at the place where Jesus was crucified, of course along with many others. This shows that your ancestors at one time lived in Israel, or around that area, and then Immigrated to Italy.

Italy is where your ancestor who is praying in the chapel is from. Over time, that family travelled from Italy through to Slovakia, where they settled. This ancestor has a pure heart of sacrifice and is Blessed and supports you well. All your ancestors supported Jesus in his time. They continued over the generations, right up to the ancestor in Italy who prays sincerely for Gods kingdom to come, which was their true desire. This is one of your good-hearted ancestors who guided you to meet the Messiah. She is now Blessed and together with many others is able to support you well within your family difficulties.

I am shown another ancestor who now is also Blessed. She had suffered in her life and, being the wife of a small family, caused resentment to be passed on to you.

I will describe her situation. Your ancestor lived around the 15th century in a small village. Everything was quite normal. She had a good-hearted husband who was a farmer. She had a few beautiful children who she absolutely loved, and all was going well. Then one day the village was raided and her husband and children were all killed. She observed them being brutally killed as she was hiding in a small area and watched everything. She made no noise and therefore was missed by the attackers. She knew that many other villagers were also killed and so she stayed hidden for several days, in case the killers returned. She slowly went out of her mind with fear and loneliness.

Over time, she came out of hiding and met up with the few remaining villagers who then helped each other survive. So many of the huts in the village were burnt to the ground. The remaining villagers managed to build new huts and life was beginning once more to get back to some normalcy, but never as before due to so many being killed.

One day your ancestor saw travelers pass through the village who had children. She was so lonely that she felt she needed to have children again to love and care for, as her own three children had been so brutally killed. Being desperate, she set out and followed that travelling family on foot. They travelled in small caravans.

She was out of her mind with loneliness and never thought about food for herself or how to survive. She began to steal and take food from the market stalls and would sleep anywhere. She spent long hours observing those families as they shopped and bought vegetables in the market. Seeing a family that had three children, she felt that she needed the youngest who was only a young baby. She felt that if she had the youngest, then the family would be okay as they would have the other two children. It was such a crazy idea that she had.

She followed the family and then, after dark, she kidnapped the baby and escaped into the forest. She found a small cave that was several kilometers away from the market town. There she settled. Finally it felt good to have a child to love. She felt spiritually driven to continue to kidnap and have two more children, as three was the number she had and lost in her own family. So, she repeated the plan over a month or so and kidnapped two more babies from two other families. She stayed in the cave where she loved and hugged the babies, but she forgot that she needed to feed them. As her mind was so damaged, all she could see was *her own* children in her arms. She would slowly rock them back and forth in her arms, but over time they slowly died of starvation.

She was not aware of what was happening and she ended up over the many months with three dead babies. Your ancestor was so out of her mind that she never recognized that they were dead and would continue to love them as if they were alive.

So, your ancestor would steal food to live but never realized she needed to feed the babies. Over several months, she lived in the cave with three dead and decaying babies. She would sit and stare in a blank way within the darkness of the cave rocking her dead babies on her lap and humming tunes she would have hummed to her own children. A farmer found her as he was working in the forest and called the authorities to the cave. Your ancestor was arrested for kidnap and murder.

Normally, your ancestor would have been hanged or put to death in some way. But, the authorities could see that she was insane, so she was committed to a mental asylum where she spent the rest of her short life as she died of loneliness and heartache. And that's what drove her insane in the end.

The parents of those babies had so much resentment towards your ancestor that they could not forgive her. Over the many generations they developed so much resentment that after their deaths they focused their strong resentment on that ancestor's descendent - that person being you.

There are other of your descendants who could have been tormented, but as you are in a position chosen by the messiah to create a new blood lineage, then you were the one to *focus on* rather than any other of your relatives.

Those resentful spirits entered your spirit and prevented your child from developing in a normal way, which is why your third child did not survive. They only chose the third child to invade because your ancestor never kidnapped the first two, only the third one from a family. She knew that to kidnap all the children, leaving the parents with no children, would be wrong. And so she would leave them with two and she would take the third one. Your ancestor caused a lot of resentment for obvious reasons. But of course she was out of her mind, having seen her own family killed before her own eyes.

She is now liberated and Blessed together with her husband. They are so grateful to you for having liberated and Blessed so many other ancestors. No words can express to you their sorrow for having caused so many resentful spirits that prevented your third child from being born.

Your ancestors know that you have paid a great price because of those resentful spirits. Your ancestors believe that your next child should be born okay and will try to support you more than they were able to before. They guided you to meet the Messiah, along with many other good religious minded ancestors. The resentful spirits, though, tormented you in the same way by having your third child killed.

A suggestion would be to attend a few liberation sessions to remove those resentful spirits, possibly to stay for three or seven days or even a long weekend, but this is only a suggestion. Your ancestors believe that your next baby should be okay, but to remove resentful spirits would be a good condition to do. God, of course, is really the only one who knows for sure.

Resentful spirits won't just go away and would appear in your children's spirit at any time if not removed. This is the sad thing about resentful spirits. They can decide when, where and with which child they want to torment. Ancestors themselves carry so many burdens. But, they are now able to be released from their torment through the liberation programs. This is the time we are living in now when all of the ancestors and spirits in the spirit world can eventually be renewed. Ancestors can be reunited with their love ones who were separated centuries ago and become Blessed, as this *one* above has been.

Husband

I can see that your spirit is also bright, radiating God's warm love which flows out past your spirit. I am allowed to observe two ancestors who, now being Blessed, have changed. But, I am allowed to see how they used to be and how they lived, the first being a monk who married later in life. This ancestor left a monastic order under instruction from heaven to marry and have children in order to pass on his religious experiences of his God-centered heart of love, dedication, compassion and sacrifice.

This monk lived around the 13th century. I see him spinning yarn to make cloth to make the 'habits' and many other garments used in the monastery. He was a good tailor who could sew and was very creative. He would also pray for hours. As he did this, he would often receive many heavenly revelations.

Another ancestor lived around the 17th century. This ancestor made garments from leather including shoes and boots. He would also receive revelations from heaven. These monks were given instructions from heaven to marry later in life in order to keep their bloodline going. They liked the idea of socializing and meet up with other relatives.

Each of these ancestors were family men who liked to entertain and meet together with other relatives. They each felt moved to live religious lives of service and sacrifice to others within normal society.

These ancestors, along with many others, helped guide you throughout your life and brought you to meet the Messiah. Your Blessed ancestors are so grateful to each of you. Even though they laid the foundation for your spiritual level of growth, you both are the ones living in the time of the Messiah.

Having sacrificed your time, energy, and a lot of money to free your ancestors so as to be together now as couples who were separated for centuries, they cannot express their gratitude to you enough.

They know that with the new truth, history has changed and is all different now. The gates of heaven have been opened and you, having been chosen to be their spearhead and representatives by God, they will therefore do everything in their power to support you. Your ancestors will work to support you, your children and their future. Your children have inherited all the good qualities from both of you, and being in a harmonious and loving family, they should continue to develop well.

This ends your reading.

Testimony – Reading 7

A couple's reading that describes their spirit level, plus a description of a few of their ancestors that have been guiding them through the years.

Husband

Looking at your photo, I entered your spirit realm. Your spirit is directly in front of me. The core of your spirit is generating strong waves of love energy, originating from the root of your spirit, and flows out to fill your whole spirit.

The top of your spiritual head is open. Flowing down from heaven is a pillar of warm light which enters through this opening in your head and blends with the bright energy of your spirit. This pillar of warm light originates from an area of the spirit world that supports heavenly spirits. These spirits can freely travel through this pillar of energy to share their inspirations and insights with you when they enter and blend with your spirit.

I see God's love blending and producing warm waves of love that flow out through your face and body, filling the area immediately around you with bright love and warmth. As I look again at your photo, I observe a male ancestor from your father's lineage. He is not yet Blessed and stands directly behind you. His looks are of an

Arabic descendant. He is tall and thin, with a beard and a turban-like cloth around his head. He wears a loose, gray gown with a cord that is tied tightly around his waist. On this cord hangs a long curved sword. His boots are made of leather. He is a nomad who wanders the desert with a large group of tribesmen, together with their families, looking for pastureland for their horses and animals to graze on.

When they find a suitable place, they settle for a few months. This ancestor lived around the 16th or 17th centuries. This same ancestor rode a black horse. He was a married man with many children and his character was reflective and internal, with a peaceful and loving appreciation for the land and nature. He would spend many long hours watching over his horses and the other animals.

His wife was very practical and down-to-earth. She was able to make cloth (some kind of weaving) to make garments for her family and community.

When your ancestor sat on his horse, his mind was peaceful. He would enter into a form of meditation. He would look far out across the vast empty land to a small line of mountain landscapes on the horizon. In the evening he would sit with his family and others around an open fire and together they would watch the sun go down. In his meditative, peaceful state he would receive many visions and could experience the presence of his ancestors. Because of these experiences, he never felt alone. His ancestors would show him things and tell him of their experiences and stories of their lives. Then, he would share those stories and visions he received with his community as they all sat together around the fire. He had a reputation of being the internal and wise one who could find answers to people's worries and questions. His children inherited his qualities of being internal and spiritually open.

Several of his children married and some emigrated to different parts of the world. They had a strong desire to see the world and to advance their lives. A couple of your ancestor's children learned to read and write and became teachers. Others became traders. They also felt a strong desire or an internal drive to find answers to many of their own questions - like the purpose of their life.

These ancestors have been the ones who searched for you and prepared you to become the spearhead of your lineages. After numerous generations, they found you and guided you to meet the Messiah. You inherited your character from your Arabic ancestor mentioned above. He was also quite laid-back, able to let time pass and feel quite content with life. This attitude can be good but in the time we are living in, this kind of character can hold you back in your restoration.

It is good to be a bit laid-back and to relax when you spend time with your family and relatives. But, you still need to remind yourself that you are living in an historic age where action is vital. Directly behind your spirit stands your couples Blessed ancestors. They stand united and radiate an intense bright wall of God's love which illuminates your whole spirit realm. They stand close to you and focus their bright love on your spirit.

You absorb your Blessed ancestor's prayers directly into your spirit which boosts and amplifies your spirit, making your spirit balanced and stable. This is one of the ways your Blessed ancestors can support you.

Wife

Looking at your photo, I entered your spirit realm. Your spirit is directly in front of me. The color of your spirit is bright white and it generates a warm glow, filling your whole spirit. The core of your spirit continuously radiates God's pure love which flows out from within you like water from a spring, flowing out of the ground.

As I continue to look at your spirit, I am taken back over several generations to a castle in the middle-ages where I see a young woman wearing mediaeval dress. She has a white cloth over her head which is held by a thin metal band that keeps it in place. She wears a long dark green dress that reaches from her shoulders to the floor. Tied around her waist hangs a loose cord with tassels at both ends. She is an ancestor from your mother's lineage who was married with children. She lived in the Castle and worked in the kitchen. She was responsible to place the different kinds of food on the long wooden tables and needed to make sure everyone had enough space to sit along benches on each side of the table. She was a head servant, maybe.

She is extremely active at meal times, rushing to bring more food and remove empty plates. She also makes sure that the younger servants keep every guest's goblet filled with wine or ale. She is a good organizer and has many responsibilities which she is able to fulfil because of her multitasking skills. She also has her own children to look after when she finds the time.

Her husband is a guard protecting the Castle, but is often called to go to battle, staying away from home for days, weeks or even months at a time. He must often leave her alone so she needs to be internally strong and motivated. She has a good female friend who is much older and who was at one time a nun. She is responsible for the education of all the children living in the Castle. Your ancestor would spend the little time she had talking with the nun, and over time she learned to focus her mind on peaceful things. This helped her through her day and enabled her to cope with her stressful life.

The nun was a really good friend who would show her how to pray for her husband when he went out to different battles. She never knew if he would return alive. Many times she would kneel in a prayer position in front of her bed, with hands together and tears running down her cheeks. Her children slept in the next room, knowing that they may never see their father again.

Her prayers brought comfort and peace, knowing and sensing that there is a better place he would go to if he should die. She felt comforted to know that she would find her husband in the next world and both could together live with God. She developed her faith in God and, together with her children, they would all sit and listen to stories from the Bible. In those times of prayer and through listening to different Bible stories she had many revelations and visitations from saints and angels, especially when she prayed with tears for her husband.

This ancestor was one of many who had been guiding you to meet the Messiah. You inherited much of her character along with her internal determination, organizational abilities plus her passionate love for her family and God. Your love for God and your family is your first love, and religion and upholding church traditions come second. Your character complements your husband's character without being too overwhelming for him. You enjoy being peaceful together as a family, but you are also able to be dynamic and will involve your family in the important traditions of our daily lifestyle.

Your attitude towards life, plus the continued support from your good-hearted ancestor described above, who is now Blessed, allows your spirit to connect to God's pure energy that never ends. Every person naturally lives half in the physical world and half in the spirit world, meaning that everyone is a spiritual being with a connection to the spirit world.

What people don't realize is that love is God himself. Everyone is spiritually open and able to communicate with the spirit world through love. The 'Principle' gave man this new truth and understanding. This simple awareness that '*love is God'* and our true parent, is able to guide mankind back to his/her true parent. This is the power of love. God's love has never deserted mankind. Many people always knew that there was something greater than themselves, which kept many searching for throughout the generations. Fortunately for each of us, the truth is finally revealed.

The top of your spiritual head is also open, similar to your husband's. A pillar of bright energy also descends from heaven and enters through your head and blends with your spirit. Both of you have a pillar of energy that originates as one single pillar that divides and then enters each of you.

This pillar of energy is a tunnel similar to an umbilical cord that is a direct connection into the higher levels of the spirit world. This is happening to both of you because of all the spiritual foundation and efforts made in your spiritual lives, and through what you inherited from your ancestors.

When you look at the paintings of saints done by the great master painters, you can see that in religious paintings the artist painted white or yellow halos around the tops of saints' heads. If you could see spiritually, you would see a pillar of energy descending from heaven that, coming to rest on the top of their heads, forms this halo. This is how spiritually open and guided many famous artists were and how God could influence their creativity. The pillar of energy enters both of your heads at the same time.

Even when you are separated it is still there, which reflects the unity of heart and love you have for one another. When you think of each other in a loving way, each of you can feel the other's presence. You are both spiritually connected through the love you have for one another. When you focus your love on each other, your love will blend. When you focus your love on your children, they will have the same experience which makes them feel secure. They will intuitively know their origin as you both resemble God to them.

Looking at the photo of your whole family sitting together on the couch, I can see the bright warm love flowing out of each of your spirits which envelopes you all, creating a wonderful heavenly atmosphere of love and harmony.

Through this love your children are naturally drawn to you both. This is so important for their emotional and spiritual development. This scene is also supported by all your Blessed ancestors' presence. This ends your reading.

Testimony - Reading 8

A spiritual reading for a couple that wants to improve their relationship. I will also describe a few of the ancestors that have been guiding them throughout their lives.

Husband

Looking at your photo I entered your spirit realm. Your spirit is directly in front of me. Your spirit looks crystal clear, almost translucent, and your Blessed ancestors are standing with you. They generate intense white waves of love that fill your whole spirit realm; you have inherited from many of your good-hearted ancestors the base for your clear spirit and your moral attitude.

They are now Blessed. I will describe one ancestor, in particular, who has been strongly influencing you and tirelessly guiding you throughout your life.

Looking again at your spirit, I am taken back many generations to 15th century Russia where I see a stocky woman in her 40's, all dressed in black. This woman is an ancestor from your mother's lineage. I see her standing together with many other women; everyone dressed in black.

She is married with children. Her husband works in the fields to support his family. His wife regularly meets together with other women from her village to pray for a better world for their children to grow up in.

They stand together in an Orthodox church that is situated outside the village, surrounded by countryside and deep in snow. The church is not heated and I can see white breath coming from the mouths of the women as they pray. Inside the church are many old paintings of Saints hanging all around the walls. An altar is at the front of the hall with a large crucifix standing on its own behind it. The crucifix has a large figure of Jesus on it.

These women are deep in prayer and they have been standing for many hours in the cold with only the warmth of the candles to give them any heat. They continue to pray without eating or drinking. Through their devotion, they purify their spirit and the atmosphere around them. Their suffering and sacrifice take them to a point where they become numb physically and mentally.

Standing in the cold for hours and fasting, combined with lack of sleep, they become cleaned out spiritually. On this foundation they received strong revelations about the second coming of the Messiah.

Their devotion opened a channel to the good spirit world and attracted a pillar of light to descend from heaven. This beautiful light would rest on the top of each woman's head.

Through this pillar of light Jesus, Angels, Saints and many visions would appear to the women, they were revelations of things to come.

You have inherited your ancestors purity of spirit, this ancestor together with many other good-hearted ancestors have been guiding you throughout your life and eventually brought you to meet the Messiah.

You also have inherited her desire to find God which gives you the urge to keep searching, even though you have been Blessed and have Blessed children.

Your desire to find God and to discover the reason why God chose you is still haunting you. Your ancestors had many revelations to prepare their descendant (you) to meet the Messiah. Now that they have achieved this, your purpose for them has changed.

They could bring you to this level but no further. Now you have the responsibility to liberate and bless all these ancestors who have guided you to this point. Their enthusiasm and devotion is limited because it is based on their understanding and faith in the Bible.

You inherited their purity and precious experiences, which has made your spirit look so translucent. They prepared the base for you to learn the new truth the Messiah brings to mankind in this new age. The Messiah comes as the master of love and he comes to unravel the mysteries and unanswered questions about God (e.g. why God created mankind and creation and so on).

You have been chosen by your ancestors to be their representatives and the spearhead, who will lead them into the new age by liberating and Blessing them.

This would show them the way to receive God's new teachings and to rid themselves of their original sin and fallen nature through the liberation Providence.

When they return to your home through the *Welcome home ancestor ceremony*, they come as Blessed couples who attended a

Blessing program; they know that.

They have removed all their old ways of thinking, old habits and religious traditions which have kept them living in a limited, narrow way. They are now free to live in this new age. The challenge for you is that for them to be able to unite with you and your family, you also need to have the same spiritual base that they have.

The struggle you are finding is that, although your ancestors have left you in order to develop a new vision and religious influence, their own past experiences are still with you.

On earth, we all live in a sea of spirits who surround us. There are many positive and negative influences of all different kinds affecting us. It can be a struggle to understand the new truth and then how to practice it. Sometimes you feel insecure and so you continue to live your ancestors' old ways.

This was good enough for your ancestors to guide you to the movement and to meet the Messiah, but not anymore.

Your Blessed ancestors have returned to you like new wine and you are like the wineskins. But, as the saying goes, "New wine must be poured into new wineskins." Luke 5:38

So you have to be on the same level as your ancestors or they cannot relate to you. This is what many members are experiencing now, even though they have Blessed 210 generations of ancestors. It is because they themselves don't feel confident how to live and practice the principle that they feel no difference internally and they doubt if there is any support from their own Blessed ancestors. This situation causes much confusion.

Your situation is like this: Your Blessed ancestors cannot blend well with your Spirit because you still live your ancestors' old inherited ways and lifestyle.

You need to change, so that your whole family can benefit from the heavenly fortune your Blessed ancestors have directly inherited from God.

Your Blessed ancestors are couples in love, and as couples they radiate intense bright waves of love which makes them look as though they are wearing holy gowns.

God is love and wants to dwell in every Blessed couple once they have rid themselves of all their fallen nature through attending the liberation programs.

To make the same base and to be able to blend with your ancestors, you need to live in love. This is achieved by sharing love in your couple, but this is not happening. Your spirit reflects the devotion of your ancestors toward living a pure life, which only focuses on the spiritual concept of God and is centered on strict religious traditions. Because of this, you are denying physical and emotional love and affection in your couple.

This attitude is reflected in your couple's relationship by your rejecting or pushing away or denying your wife's emotional advances of love towards you, giving her the feeling that you do not love her.

This comes from the old religious traditions you inherited from your ancestors. Before their Blessing, your ancestors put up a strong resistance toward receiving love. To deny physical love and emotional closeness may have been needed in the past, but not anymore. Now you need to focus on the emotional love in your couple to be able to fulfill your Blessing. The reason is that God is both Love and our True Parent.

We are all born through our parents love. We grow through the love of our parents. We then receive the Blessing in order to share love with our spouse. Together in love, a wife and husband create children to whom they can give their love; love being the reason for life.

Because so many ancestors have been liberated from your spirit, their influence on you is now very weak because your focus was never really on the physical and emotional aspect of your relationship. You don't know how emotionally free you are.

Even without your ancestor's influences, you still resist and reject love. It should not take you very long to free your emotions and be able to give love to your wife, once you try, since the base for your problems has been removed and your ancestors have moved on.

Your couple can blend in love on earth and in the spirit world. You will have everything if you have love. If you don't love each other, you will be separated in the spirit world.

You will both live as single people in a different spirit realm for eternity, or until someone from your Blessed ancestors comes to invite you to a liberation program where you will be reunited with your love ones and your lives can begin to change for the better.

Wife

Looking at your photo, I entered your spirit realm. Your spirit is directly in front of me and the color of your spirit is bright and sparkling white.

Your Blessed ancestors stand around you and radiate an intense bright white energy that illuminates your whole spirit realm.

Looking deep into your spirit, I see warm love filling your whole spirit which radiates out into your spirit realm. Your ancestors stand closely around you but they don't blend with your spirit. This is because the level they are on is different from your level, even though you are a Blessed couple.

You inherited attitudes, habits and standards from your ancestors who guided you throughout your life to keep you on the right track to eventually meet the Messiah. To do this, your ancestors had to deny and reject any emotional love and instead only focused on their religious devotion and faith. This has allowed them to be close to you. But now they are Blessed. They have removed those old traditions and attitudes towards emotional love because they know that God is the essence of love; God is love.

I will describe one particular ancestor from whom you inherited your main outlook on life and who is now causing you to struggle.
Looking at your spirit, I am taken back over many generations to a large village in Mongolia. It is around the 13th century. Situated at the center of this village is a large Buddhist temple. A young girl from your mother's lineage is leaving the temple, followed by her mother and grandmother. Many other women followed them inside to the center of the temple where there stands a great hall. Inside this hall lays an old man who is related to the Emperor, but he is dying...
Your ancestors, together with many other women, have all been kneeling for hours, praying for the health of this old and sick man. Your ancestors were prayer women who would pray for the well-being of the Emperor.
This kind of 'job' has been handed down from mother to daughter over many generations. The youngest daughter was being trained in the prayer traditions of the Palace and when she qualifies she will join the rest of the prayer women.

Every day they would spend many hours in prayer, love and

devotion. Their lives were disciplined, which reflected in the ancestors of those times. They all had peaceful, calm and creative natures.

Their prayers would attract many good ancestors and good spirits to come to them, and this would block out the negative spirits who tried to enter the temple where the atmosphere was calm. Some of your good-hearted ancestors who brought you to meet the Messiah were allowed to marry and have children, mainly for the sake of keeping the lineage of prayer women going.

Their love and devotion was only to the Emperor; not to their husbands who were guards to protect the temple and the Emperor's family. These good-hearted ancestors who guided you to meet the Messiah could see from the spirit world a new age forming and they wanted to be a part of this exciting development.

But, they could not realize or imagine how different and challenging this new time would be for them. Your ancestors did not realize that the new age came with a new truth, this being the Divine Principle, which brought a completely new understanding of how to relate to God as a parent.

Your ancestors never understood they were children of God. They never had such a simple understanding because they were connected to divine spirit which was based only on faith alone and was only in a receiving position, similar to young children.

Now these ancestors are Blessed and all of their old ways, habits and traditions and how to have faith in God have been changed. Now they relate to God as their parent. Through the Divine Principle education and Blessed family programs, they have been brought to a new level of realization that has transformed them into truly Blessed couples where God can dwell.

Your emotional struggle is very similar to your husband's struggle, in that both your lineages of ancestors have moved on spiritually and the ancestors have removed all their old ways of thinking and any traditions that block them. They listened to the Divine Principle and attended countless liberation sessions which removed all their old habits, traditions, and fallen history. They then became Blessed and returned to your home.

They have changed and can now relate to God directly. The problem is that the character and value you inherited from them is now blocking you from being able to blend with your Blessed ancestors and become close to them. You will need to remove their old influences from you which you can only do through the liberation sessions and also sharing and focusing your desire of love, physical and emotional love towards your husband. Doing this will, over time, remove your ancestors' old influence because your ancestors are not reinforcing their old values anymore.

This will mean that you can share new romantic experiences of passion and love with your husband. These experiences should quickly replace your inherited, instinctive tendencies to reject and push away any love you are feeling. Please embrace your feelings of love, and remember that you meet God in your couple through allowing this to happen.

It will take some time and practice for you to feel comfortable to express your emotions of love. Those feelings of love and desire to be with your husband are normal. Please do not give up, even if it is difficult, but keep on going. As soon as you begin to share your love in your couple, God and your Blessed ancestors, who are one in love, will be able to blend with your spirit and support your emotions of love.

This is the reason the Blessing is so important because you can only truly experience the fullness of God's love through expressing and sharing your sexual, emotional love between you and your husband. The oneness of husband and wife is the expressed sexual, emotional love that totally reflects Gods masculine and feminine aspect.

Through shared love, God can digest any negative spirits that are causing trouble for your couple. Also, based on love, you can communicate with the spirit world where your Blessed ancestors dwell. Love is the bridge between the two worlds.

God is love and our True Parent, God, will support you 100%. So please feel confident to share and express your love in your couple.

My suggestion to help your situation would be to do a 'washing each other' condition. This will stimulate your passion and desire for each other and release your inner emotions for each other. This will attract God and your Blessed ancestors to enter and occupy your couple's spirit.

Another suggestion would be to read the Cheong Seong Gyeong book, chapters 9, 10 and 11, which talk about man's true origin and the sexual organ being the dwelling place of God. This will give you confidence and more reassurance to get emotionally closer to each other.

If you would like to know more about this suggested book, then please contact me, the author of this reading. This ends your reading.

Testimony - Reading 9

A reading for a couple to discover the root of some illnesses within the family

Husband

Looking at your photo I entered your spirit realm. Your spirit is directly in front of me. Your spirit has a bright energy that generates from the root of your spirit which is just below your navel.

God's energy enters your spirit at that point and radiates out, filling your spirit. As this happens, some of your bright vitality elements are absorbed by a few resentful spirits that surround and lean into your spirit.

Your Blessed ancestors that I can see stand back, allowing those resentful spirits to immediately surround your spirit and blend into your spirit. These resentful spirits are there because of how a few

of your ancestors treated others when they lived on earth.

I am shown one of the ancestors that caused some of those resentful spirits that have accumulated over many generations by your different ancestors.

As I look into your spirit, I am taken back many centuries and shown an ancestor who is now Blessed and together with his wife who supports you. I am allowed to observe how that ancestor's character was, and what he did to cause those spirits to become resentful.

I see a male ancestor living in the 13th century. He was part of an army; a simple soldier who along with many others invaded and killed villagers. This was common in those days and your ancestor was part of a group of men who were in charge of interrogating prisoners.

In a Castle where they were based, he was the main interrogator. His job was to get information out of prisoners. He did not kill many men or women in the villages which they raided, but he was good at getting information out of prisoners.

One method of torture to gain information from prisoners was to stretch their neck. This was done by hanging the prisoner in a 'stock,' which was two pieces of stout wood which could be separated and with a half-hole facing each other in each side. This wooden device would be put around the prisoner's neck and then closed; the prisoner was then hoisted up so their feet were off the ground, similar to rope hanging.

The head was the only thing suspending the body as the prisoner's hands were tied behind their back. Being suspended by the head stretched the nerves in the spine and crushed the eardrums. This would cause so much pressure on the chin and the neck that it caused blood to come out of their eyes.

The ears were also ruptured. If prisoners survived, they would struggle with hearing loss and possibly blindness. The nerves in the neck could easily be stretched to the point where they would break, and so the person would be paralyzed from the neck down.

This was, of course, if the prisoner survived. He could be suspended like that for days, or until he revealed all the information that was needed. Many men died this way.

As those people entered the spirit world they could see your ancestor, and seeing that they themselves were still alive spiritually, they became resentful and filled with so much hate.

Over the years those spirits tormented your ancestors through nightmares and bad dreams, even appearing in his children's dreams, causing them different forms of mental problems and disabilities.

Not all of them, but at least one ancestor over each generation, was influenced this way. This was the impact of one of those resentful spirits that are now influencing you.

I am then shown another ancestor who is also Blessed, but this is a very different quality of ancestor. He was a farmer who was married and living in the 15th century. He would meditate as he worked in the fields. Many times he would receive revelations from heaven that he would need to be ready for the time when the Anointed One would return to save the world.

His own ancestors would appear, surrounding him as he would put seeds in the earth, as he planted his crops. His ancestors would appear to him as see-through translucent white images and would speak to him, as your (the husband's) ancestor was quite open spiritually.

He often had visitations from angels and visions that told him, "You need to be ready for when the Chosen One comes." He asked them when that would happen, but they did not know. They said he would be told when the time came.

He was also told that he needed to learn about Jesus and the Saints and how they lived. He should be taught by a monk how to read and write. This was the preparation needed to recognize the Chosen One.

Your ancestor then told his wife and children who were

surprisingly supportive. So, he visited a monastery that was not so far away and asked if a monk could visit their home every two weeks or once-a-month to educate them.

Of course a monk would come. Your ancestor would pay him for his services with food from his farm. One year there was a problem growing food as there was a shortage of water. Your ancestor would help those living close-by, giving food for free to many that would otherwise have starved.

He helped so many of the villagers survive. This was one of your many good-hearted and religious-minded ancestors who have helped guide you to meet the Messiah. He now stands together with his wife, along with many other Blessed ancestors who continue to support you in the spirit world.

Resentful spirits, though, are blocking your Blessed ancestors from totally blending with your spirit and they need to be removed. I am sure you have removed very many through the liberation sessions, but there are still some left. When they are removed, your relationship with your wife will emotionally improve.

Those spirits also create a weakness in your physical body. Through your immune system Malaria affects your blood system.

Many resentful spirits enter through the top of your head and are digested in the stomach, similar to how food in your physical body is digested. Tension caused by resentful spirits can be seen as intestinal blockages or liver problems. When those resentful spirits are removed, those problems you experience will affect you much less.

Your son will also benefit as the problems he suffers with have been inherited from your ancestors. Those resentful spirits are tormenting your son in the same way they were themselves killed.

Those departed prisoners that are in the spirit world died because of those problems caused by your ancestor. Now they want to torment your son the same way they were tormented and have chosen your son as he is the second-born.

He stands in the 'Abel' position within your family. If those spirits had been allowed to attack you and influenced your spirit and body, you would have had real difficulty to meet the Messiah and become Blessed. You may not have even met our movement. The struggles then that you would have been put through would have been quite difficult. But, there was a program for your restoration as a family and the reason why you are now Blessed and have been brought together in this special time.

What is happening in your family was allowed to happen. Later, only after you could start the Providence of Restoration helping the Messiah by creating a new blood lineage, would those resentful spirits be allowed to surface through your second child.

The second child acts like a conduit, channeling those resentful spirits out through him. As you remove those resentful spirits from yourself, you will also remove them from your son as he is younger than 12 years old.

As a lot of the physical damage may have been done already to your son's health, it may not be totally possible to heal those problems completely.

Those resentful spirits want to make your life as difficult as possible. So, your son is taking a very important position to protect your family. However, as those spirits are removed, then both his and your health should begin to improve.

If there is a lot of physical damage, it may not be possible to completely improve. But, by removing those resentful spirits, they won't come out in future generations.

If your son can manage to get Blessed after those resentful spirits have been removed, then they won't come out through his children. This is what is possible through removing resentful spirits. They would be removed from his spirit and so not be passed on to future generations. And also, when your son goes to the spirit world he won't have those physical limitations. But that is far into the future.

He is just acting as a conduit at this moment in your family's restoration program. This is a process through which those resentful spirits can be channeled and removed by the liberation sessions.

Mother

Looking at your photo I entered your spirit realm. Your spirit is directly in front of me. Your spirit radiates strong vitality elements. God's energy flows into your spirit. Your Blessed ancestors stand close to your spirit and blend with your bright energy that radiates out past your spirit body.

Looking at your spirit, I am taken back over several generations to the 15th century where I am shown a 'now Blessed' ancestor. I am allowed to observe your ancestors' lives before they became 'Blessed ancestors' so that you can see who you inherited your characteristics from.

I am shown a Gypsy from a nomadic Romany family who travelled through Europe in caravans made of wood – a Vardo. They lived off the land.

Your ancestor, having a strong influence on your life, was the wife who has a strong husband. They travelled around as relatives' altogether. These are your side lineages. But, the one I am describing is from your own direct lineage. She had several children whom she 'schooled' from home.

She was an herbalist who could create remedies for health by mixing different flowers and herbs. She was open spiritually and could feel the presence of energy from trees and plants.

She could also recognize problems in people when she looked at them, and would always prepare a remedy to help them. She would also receive revelations from heaven through dreams and visions. She would often be guided to important herbs and to certain mystical places to camp where the best atmosphere was found.

This ancestor was not traditionally religious but had a deep belief in the afterlife. She could sense the spirit world and the energy from the universe.

This ancestor, along with many others, guided you to meet the Messiah. I am not observing many resentful spirits that are influencing you, so I won't talk about them.

Your 'couple' blends quite well together and God can work through you well. If you can continue removing any of the resentful spirits that surround you through the liberation sessions, it will make life in your family that much more harmonious, plus help improve your entire family's health.

If too much damage is already done, as I explained before, then your son's health may not be able to improve that much. However, at last those resentful spirits that have been following your ancestral lineages and passing down through to your descendants will have been removed.

Any visit to attend a liberation session will benefit your family. You will know how long to stay as you feel things improve, which will give you a good indication.

We always have so many resentful spirits to remove, but it shouldn't take long to remove those most troublesome spirits as I can see them very easily. This means they are very exposed and close to the surface so they should be able to leave quite quickly.

This concludes your reading.

Testimony - Reading 10

A spiritual reading to reveal what is happening in a person's spirit realm.

As I look into your spirit realm I observe some of your ancestors and spirits, all having an influence on your life today. Many spirits come to you as a result of your ancestors' deeds, both good and bad. The question is how we can return to our original position so that everyone, including those in the spirit world, can freely share joy with our Heavenly Parent in true love.

As I looked at your photo, I entered your spirit realm. Your spirit is directly in front of me. As I look at your spirit I observe one of your ancestors from your great-grandmother's lineage who has an influence on you.

She was the wife of a tribal leader living in the region of Botswana during the 16th century. She and her husband spent a lot of their time in their hut made of sticks and mud, and they would hold consultations for villagers who came to them for advice.

They would sometimes use incense to purify the atmosphere in their hut. As a result, your ancestor would spend much time in a trance (a meditative state-of-mind) experimenting with and testing the spirit world and other dimensions of consciousness.

One day your ancestor had a spiritual experience in which the spirit world opened up to her much more clearly than ever before and she saw her ancestors, relatives (side lineages like aunt/uncle, nephew/niece, cousin..), and other spirits -- hundreds of thousands -- all dancing in joy around a statue of two people holding hands. But the faces of the statue were not shown. Your ancestor recognized this statue to represent two people in the future whom she called "the new ones," who were to come and release everyone from their suffering on the earth.

The main motivation for carrying out her spiritual experiences was that she could feel the world was somehow "broken" and she felt a deep sense of urgency to '*find a way to fix it.*' Your ancestor's husband, the tribal leader, would listen to his wife when she shared her experiences with the spirit world.

She was his guide and mentor. Occasionally, he would ask her for guidance such as how to lead his tribe or when people came to him for advice. His wife would not comment or say anything in front of others. She would not question her husband in public or when the people were with them. She would stay obediently silent and instead observe quietly, with patience and admiration.

She knew that her husband was the tribal leader and that the people respected him that way. They also respected him because they saw how he honored his wife.

Only when they both were alone would the husband ask his wife what she thought of the guidance he gave to the people. She would advise him based on her spiritual experiences and intuition. She had a very important role to fulfil; more than just having concern for public recognition. The people did not know exactly how she helped her husband, but this did not worry her. She received love and protection from her husband, who stood between her and the community.

Your ancestor left a ‘messianic hope’ and expectation in your family history.

She would share her testimonies with members of her own family who already knew from childhood that she experienced the spirit world. Later on she would have more spiritual experiences. She would spend more and more time in nature, learning the value and beauty of giving and receiving love with the creation.

Her messianic hope and expectation, which was different from others (based on the statue of the couple), was passed on in her community with the help of her husband who stood in the middle between the two.

This influenced other families for the good, and much good fortune was added to your lineage. This could be picked up later on by other descendants.

Your ancestor and her husband worked well as a couple and they set the foundation for a pattern that could be followed and passed on to their descendants later on.

Years later, ancestors in your Mother's lineage began migrating out of the Botswana region, crossing threatening rivers on their way through the searing heat. The rivers, though not
always deep, had very strong currents and your ancestors could have easily been washed away. They had to ensure they had their feet firmly on the ground as they walked through the unclear waters. They were not able to see their next step, so they walked cautiously yet confidently on the foundation of each previous step. The blue dress you are wearing in your photo resembles the struggle your ancestors went through as they overcame troubling waters during their migration.

The white jacket you are wearing in the photo represents the good works of your ancestors, who have been lovingly and laboriously guiding your lineage from the spirit world.

They hoped that the inspiration they offered their descendants on the earth would bring beautiful fruits quickly. These fruits have been realized in your family, in your generation, through your Blessing and your children.

Your migrating ancestors eventually settled in Zambia.
During the 1860's, when one of your female ancestors from your Mother's lineage was in her mid-20's, she met a Christian missionary and became evangelized.
This was around the same time David Livingstone was in Zambia. He died there, too.
This ancestor became a Christian and thus brought your lineage in line with God's providence when she accepted and started to believe in Jesus as the Messiah.
Your ancestor would often pray and would receive special revelations from the spirit world which was connected with the historical merit your earlier ancestors set as they educated their tribal people. She taught about the future and the coming of the "new ones", which was a messianic hope for the future.
In one such revelation, your ancestor saw and listened to many thousands of angels, singing praises to God with the expectation of the Second Coming of Christ. She saw this and hoped that the Second Coming of Christ could be realized in her lifetime.
But it would not be realized until after her time had come and gone.
This kind of situation, her being alive in between the lifetimes of the first and second comings of the Messiah, caused much sorrow in her heart.

Your ancestor's heartfelt prayers to attend the Messiah caused merit that was passed down through the lineage, and thus it came out in you.

This ancestor laid the foundation for you to meet the Messiah in your lifetime and to receive the Blessing. Although your ancestor never met the Messiah in her lifetime, she could see the coming of the new age from the spirit world and eagerly prompted you to follow it.

Through the ancestor Liberation and Blessing Providence of Cheongpyeong, our ancestors can be liberated and Blessed by God. Blessed ancestral couples find it easier to blend with a Blessed couple on earth. It is this love, based on unity in the Blessed couple, which is God's love. On the foundation of this love, your Blessed ancestors are able to blend with your couple to help you directly. Otherwise, you might not be able to have complete give-and-take with them.

Another of your ancestors, a man who lived in the early 18th century, belongs to your Father's lineage. He is Congolese and worked for white European slave traders in his country. This ancestor was a language interpreter. He translated conversations between European slave traders and local African tribal leaders. These tribal leaders sold their own people as slaves to the European slave traders. Your ancestor had a privileged and protected position. He was valued for his communication ability.

This ancestor did not receive many threats from slave traders, but he knew that if he did not do his job well, the slave traders would destroy his inheritance (land and property) and they would kill him or his whole family.

So, your ancestor worked hard to satisfy the slave traders; to keep his family safe that he loved dearly. Many times your ancestor went in secret to help the slave traders collect new slaves from local tribal leaders.

For this, many African natives from 18th century resent and hate your ancestor very much. They say he betrayed them. This ancestor caused a lot of rage and resentment in his lifetime.

In the 1720's, another tribal man fought back against the slave traders and your ancestor tried to capture him, working together with the slave traders. They were going to sell him to people in another country.

But this native resisted. He fought back and eventually was killed by the slave traders and your ancestor during a struggle with a blow struck to his head. This man had a wife and children. Unfortunately, this man's daughter witnessed the fight between her father and your ancestor. She saw the slave traders and your ancestor kill her father. This daughter holds very much anger and resentment toward your ancestor. She says her father was murdered. With such resentment the daughter, who is still now a resentful spirit, tried very hard to separate your couple.

She thinks: "If I can't be with my father, why should her child (your son as a descendant of your ancestor who killed her father) be with his father?" She was seven years old when she saw her father die.

She thinks if she cannot be with her father, your son cannot be with his father, either. In the spirit world things do not change with time because in the spirit world there is a different concept of time.

Her resentment has not changed. To her it feels the same now as it did when she first arrived in the spirit world. This means she still feels the same strong desire to satisfy her resentment, which has not become less and has definitely not gone away. Even though she is only one spirit, the tendency of a resentful spirit is to attract and entice other resentful spirits to get involved in causing the pain to

others, thus multiplying the evil act.
Her resentful spirit got other spirits involved in attacking you. This resentful daughter remains with you and would like to separate you from your son still. But, you cannot allow her to do this.
All of the past fallen history of resentment caused by your ancestors can end with you.

Thanks to the arrival of the Messiah, who comes to resolve fallen history, we have the Holy Blessing Marriage Ceremony which removes original sin, and the Cheongpyeong Providence which helps to restore the mistakes our ancestors committed in the past.
Through living a principled lifestyle and forming principle-centered habits, centered on true love, we let our original nature shine and eventually absolute goodness will fill our lives.
You have liberated and Blessed some of your ancestors. But you also need to resolve the resentment your ancestors caused through attending the liberation sessions. Looking again at your spirit realm, I could see that you are a gentle and soft-natured person who wants to always think highly of others.
You are a heavenly person who believes in the good in others, but you feel pressure like a weight on you. This weight is the resentment your ancestors have caused to other spirits who want to attack you.

Gratefully, we are living in a time when we are able to liberate and bless our ancestors and resolve the resentments caused by them by removing and getting rid of those resentful spirits. Liberating and Blessing our ancestors is important, but equally important is to resolve the suffering of resentful spirits that affect us.

By participating in the liberation program, you are able to remove many generations of evil spirits who would otherwise continue to cause problems for you and your family.

You are the spearhead of your ancestors and they chose you to stop all the negative fallen history of the past from being passed on to your descendants.

This ends your spiritual reading.

Note from the author, Philip Hill

Everyone will go to the spirit world at the end of their lives. That we end up in the spirit world is a fact. The question is, where in the spirit world will we go and how will our lives here on the earth affect our life there? To understand the principles and laws of the physical world and the spirit world and how to apply them in your daily life is the answer.

If this book has stimulated your interest to find out more about the content of this book together with the meaning of the *Divine Principle* and how those principles can be applied in your daily life plus learn the meanings of words and references used in this volume such as:

Cheongpyeong Campus

Liberation ceremony

Blessing ceremony

Plus many others

Please contact the supplier or the person who introduced you to this book who will be able to send through to you further information.

Thank you.

Printed in Great Britain
by Amazon

66459190R00149